T0072290

ALSO BY
DAXTON PAGE

Side Hustle Starter-Kit
Band Progress Workbook
Masters in the Making

All of the above can be ordered by visiting:
www.DaxtonPage.com

THE
MUSICIAN'S
DILEMMA

MUSIC BUSINESS SECRETS
FOR BECOMING A MUSIC ENTREPRENEUR AND
BALANCING YOUR ART WITH YOUR BUSINESS

DAXTON PAGE

BALBOA.PRESS
A DIVISION OF HAY HOUSE

Copyright © 2022 Daxton Page.

All rights reserved. No part of this book may be used or reproduced by any means, graphic, electronic, or mechanical, including photocopying, recording, taping or by any information storage retrieval system without the written permission of the author except in the case of brief quotations embodied in critical articles and reviews.

Balboa Press books may be ordered through booksellers or by contacting:

Balboa Press
A Division of Hay House
1663 Liberty Drive
Bloomington, IN 47403
www.balboapress.com
844-682-1282

Because of the dynamic nature of the Internet, any web addresses or links contained in this book may have changed since publication and may no longer be valid. The views expressed in this work are solely those of the author and do not necessarily reflect the views of the publisher, and the publisher hereby disclaims any responsibility for them.

The author of this book does not dispense medical advice or prescribe the use of any technique as a form of treatment for physical, emotional, or medical problems without the advice of a physician, either directly or indirectly. The intent of the author is only to offer information of a general nature to help you in your quest for emotional and spiritual well-being. In the event you use any of the information in this book for yourself, which is your constitutional right, the author and the publisher assume no responsibility for your actions.

Any people depicted in stock imagery provided by Getty Images are models, and such images are being used for illustrative purposes only.
Certain stock imagery © Getty Images.

Cover design: Daxton Page
Interior design: Daxton Page
Interior illustrations: Daxton Page

Print information available on the last page.

ISBN: 979-8-7652-3432-7 (sc)
ISBN: 979-8-7652-3741-0 (hc)
ISBN: 979-8-7652-3433-4 (e)

Balboa Press rev. date: 12/07/2022

This book is dedicated to the musicians whom I have been called to serve: my "MoneySmart Musicians." You've made it possible for me to do work that interests me and that I feel is meaningful and worthwhile. The first book in my Musicians trilogy is about breaking down the myths and false beliefs about becoming a music entrepreneur so you can start to create the life you really want. If this book helps one musician overcome the dilemma and create the freedom needed to have the life they want, then this work will have been a success.

Contents

Preface

When the first singer for my first band KIRRA died in a car accident, I had a moment where I was certain my career was over. We had worked for almost 5 years building a reputation and an audience with his specific style, and losing a lead singer is one of the hardest things to overcome as a band.

Those 5 years were a grind of touring, playing shows (a lot of them close to empty), begging for labels only to end up bickering with them about how long a verse is. My band members and I come from south side of Oklahoma City, and there aren't a lot of opportunities for musicians. Somehow we managed to create our own opportunities by working hard for years on end to make a name for ourselves, and when Jesse died, it was like watching a door slowly close forever in front of you unless you do something about it.

Luckily we found our singer Gabe, and then I discovered how we could take a different approach than the last 5 years. There was a way that we could retain control over our music business, and still get our name out there and keep what we had fought for and earned with our heart, sweat, and tears. It would be a complete fresh start.

I knew there had to be a better way to operate a music business! I was 2-3 years into a journey of self-transformation when Jesse died. I was buying books like crazy on everything from investing, real estate, and business to psychology, personal development, and time management. I had been learning the foundations of entrepreneurship and how I was going to use that vehicle to create the life I wanted.

I wanted to be able to create my art in peace, but also have a career with it. I wanted the bills to be taken care of, but I didn't want to stress over my songwriting to keep food on the table. Some call this wanting your cake and to eat it to, but I never understood that saying. The purpose of cake is to be eaten, life to be lived, and artists to create. Including create the lives we want to live. Some of us want just enough to keep the bill collectors away, and give you a little comfort to do what you want to do. Other may want a little more of the extravagance that exists out there in life, and the best part is there is no wrong answer.

There is nothing wrong with wanting an abundant life. In fact, if you want to attract an abundant life, you'll have to start with an abundant mindset. Make peace with the fact you want more out of life. On the flip side, if you want to think about making just enough then that is fine as well. I would be willing to bet however, that once you reach a certain level of achievement, you will want to get to your next level.

This book is how artists can start to learn to balance the fundamentals of business with the passion and creativity of their music. You've got music that you're passionate about, but you can't let some of the noise of society today hold you back and instill false beliefs about what it means to be a successful artist. You'll hear me talk about about "art" and the philosophy around having art and business work together. This is all designed to give you a perspective that will help you maintain a great relationship with your art.

I also knew I wanted to include some great tactics for music entrepreneurs trying to have more success inside of their music business. It's one thing to balance your art and your business, but what if you don't really have much of a music business built yet? Well, have no fear! I've got you covered.

This book is going to give you insights and strategies that took over a decade of trial and error to discover, and hopefully save you from making the same mistakes and capitalize on the same strategies that worked for me!

If only one artist out there started to feel more at peace with becoming a music entrepreneur without any false beliefs attached so they could just pursue music with all of their soul, then I will have accomplished my mission. I've been in this business since I was about 15 years old, and in that time I've seen so much and learned so many lessons that would help artists out there have more success and peace within their music business—or their lives more generally.

I knew that creating this book would help musicians all over the world start to have a sense of clarity when it comes down to turning your music into a career and starting to balance all your work in your music business with the art you create. I know some people maybe scared to start becoming more of an entrepreneur because they feel that it will somehow change their relationship with their art.

I designed this book exclusively to maintain your relationship with your art in a way that is still productive to your music career. Most people seem to think it's one or the other and there's no middle in between. Well I'm here to let you know there is a way to have a career in music without letting the music industry start changing and manipulating your art.

I remember the first time I knew it was possible to not work a 9-5 job or be a starving artist while pursuing my music career. I was working at a big corporate music store where they offered lessons as well. When I got that job I signed on as an instructor who taught guitar, bass, and drums. I worked there for 3 and a half years and had an average paycheck of around $400 - $500 for the entire duration of my 3 and a half years there.

I've always wanted to work for myself and not have to spend 30 to 40 hours a week at a job where I wasn't in control of my destiny, and there was little to no room for growth. I decided to make the shift and jump into the deep end of entrepreneurship by starting my own little side hustle.

I decided the easiest way to make this transition was to go from a music instructor at a big corporate music store to a local music instrument and business teacher. It was almost exactly what I was doing for years and I had built an audience of people who wanted to learn not only how to play their instrument but how to make a career from their talent as well.

You'll hear more about this later, but my first month made me $1,317 and I had only worked 28 hours the entire month! This is when I knew that creating the freedom to create the life we want was more in our grasps that we knew. If we could imagine the way forward, we could start to take action to create and manifest our own destiny. Not the destiny others have set forth for us, but the destiny we always knew was possible — we just didn't know how.

Until now...

Now in the new digital age, it has never been more possible for a musician to build the life they want. Whether you want to live like that "*The Office*" character, Dwight Shrute and make $80,000 and year and live on a beet farm, or you want a lavish house with all the fun toys and donate unreasonable amounts of money. All of these are possible based on what *you* decide is the best move forward.

Not every musician is shooting for the exact same life, we're all different. In this day and age, you can create that life for yourself. It will take learning new things, it will be tough, you're going to run into unexpected obstacles, but the best part is you are more than capable of what it takes. Sometimes we get a bunch of thoughts and beliefs about becoming a professional musician or artist, that we start to believe that BS the people who aren't pursuing the dream we have give to us.

Hopefully this book will help you work through this dilemma and come out the other side with a gameplay to start your music career and the mindsets and principles you'll need along your journey as a career musician. This journey takes the shift from being a hobbyist into an entrepreneur, balancing your art and your business, and ultimately taking your place in this business.

Are you ready?

Let's go.

Introduction

From a surface level view, it doesn't make much logical sense to be a professional musician. There isn't a lot of short-term income potential in the business, there's an unbelievable amount of competition, and the factors that play into a successful band are much more than a group's or individual's ability to write great music.

There are thousands if not millions of teenagers, young adults, and mature adults who want to pursue music as a professional career. Yet, very few of them take their dream seriously and even fewer of those who take their dream seriously *actually* act on their dream. Why is that?

Well, this is what I call *the Musicians Dilemma*, a feeling of deep almost spiritual connection to music and the need to create and share it, but having been raised in a culture and a world that is increasingly hostile to entrepreneurs (in the face of how much it relies on them), and by consequence, lack the necessary tools to take control of their financial futures and achieve financial freedom.

This is the disease, and I'm hoping to offer the beginnings or at least a part of the cure. Professional musicians as a group of people are in a vulnerable position right now and need the mindsets, habits, and strategies of successful entrepreneurs to not only understand the business that they are in, but understand the reality of the business-world as a whole and how they can navigate and thrive within it, and create the lives for themselves they've always wanted.

I'm not here to coddle your perceptions of what this business is and what it is not, nor will I sugar coat what business in general is like. I've seen too many artists ripped off first-hand to infantilize you by giving you stories that distort your perspectives from the truth. I'll go ahead an apologize now if some of what I tell you is a bit uncomfortable or shocking for you to hear.

Like I said, I'm going to give you the cold hard truth about business, art, and things of the like. If you'd prefer to stay in the matrix, then close this book or turn off the audiobook. If you're ready to be unplugged and actually see what its truly like trying to be a professional artist, then let's go.

Let's get something straight though, if you're reading this you're most likely a musician who is serious about becoming successful and actually making a name for yourself. You need to understand that NO ONE can take away from you what you have, and that is the gift of the ability to share and create music.

There is a reason that religions, for example, all over the world use song in conjunction with their prayers and worship, it's because there is something spiritual about music. Even to the most hardcore punk or metal atheist, they will go to a concert and act out as well as be apart of an event indistinguishable from a religious gathering.

Think about it: your alter is your stage, the lead singer is the preacher (I know a lot of singers are probably not going to like that comparison), music is the spirit, and the audience is the congregation. Music is an incredibly special thing and literally can be a vehicle of transformation (for better or worse). I've seen countless stories of people telling artists that their music saved their lives.

You need to always remember why you are doing this. It could be that special relationship you have with the music itself. It could be the feeling of give and take when performing for an audience that is present with you and interacting.

I remember a time when I was on tour with KIRRA back in 2019, and we had just been driving for about 10 hours straight to get to the city we needed to keep on schedule. We are no strangers to the motel chains of America. We have seen every Super 8 known to man at this point, Wyndham hotels should sponsor us. When we got our luggage up to the room, I noticed our YouTube channel had a notification we needed to take a look at.

I saw a comment on a audio visualizer video of my band's song

"Sixteen Suns", and the comment was saying that they really needed to hear the lyrics at that time in their life and it helped her out greatly. I remember having a the hope when we wrote that song, that someone would hear those lyrics and be overcome with a sense of peace. These are the moments that bring you the greatest amounts of gratitude, and remind you the impact and value that your skills provide for people.

Whatever your reasons are for being a professional, you need to tap into those emotions on a regular basis to remind you what path you are on. This will help provide clarity in your times of trouble or anxiety.

However, we have to be extremely cautious. It is very easy for the ego of the artist to conflate itself with the primal transformative force that is music. I don't think most musicians actually understand this power nor do we treat this responsibility with the care and dignity it deserves.

Don't get me wrong, I feel strongly musicians should be able to create the music that fulfills them the most. All I'm suggesting is that every right is intrinsically associated with a responsibility, and to be a truly thoughtful and professional musician, you need to not only consider your right to make whatever music you'd like, but the responsibility and understanding that your creation could be a vehicle of transformation for somebody and you do not want to transform someones life for the worse out of your own vanity. The Marvel comic Spiderman said it best,

"...with great power comes great responsibility".
—Uncle Ben

You can't control how everyone perceives or interprets your music, and inevitably there will be people who misuse your music for *their* own vanity. We will talk about this more later in this book...

For now, I need to dive into the concept of being unbalanced. This is where I started out and where I would assume most musicians reading this are at right now. We have been raised in unbalance, so it's hardly surprising that we most likely start out from this position. However, that does not mean we are destined to be unbalanced.

Being Unbalanced

"All About The Art"   "All About The Money"

If you take the time to analyze certain aspects out your personality, you can start to see where your weaknesses are and where your strengths are. This process of self-awareness is one of the first steps to balancing both your art and your business, without it you will be pulled by unconscious forces that will pull you in directions counter-productive to your goal.

In this book, you will learn not only how to recognize your own imbalances and correct them, but be able to hopefully see it in the people around you so you will know when you are surrounded by people who are on the same mission as you. You'll also be able to figure out the strategies on how to achieve balance of your art and your business, without falling prey to many faulty notions or opinions about what it means to be an artist or what it means to be in business.

When it comes down to it, most musicians have been lied to and believe these lies because the comfort of feeling certain about an issue is more pleasing than the pain of having to admit you've been wrong about something and have to change your mind when confronted with new evidence.

The idea that artists can't make any money without "selling out" is a lie. The idea that to ask for money from your fans makes you greedy is a lie. The idea that if you want to make it big then you have to be signed by a big label (or any label for that matter) is a lie. The idea that touring is where all the money is and if you aren't touring you're losing is a lie. The idea that if you just put on a great show that your merch table will sell out is a lie.

All of these false preconceived notions about this business have been fed to us via culture. A culture that has been condemning entrepreneurs for centuries, a culture that wants to keep money and power exactly where it is and will lie to you in order to keep you confused and keep you where you're at.

I remember when I was in high school and we had to take the class "Personal Financial Literacy", and it was a 5 month class—not even a whole year. We weren't taught anything valuable about money. It taught us how to sign a check, and that's about it. It was literally the only thing they were trying to teach us. This is the system that musicians spend the first, and most formative, parts of their lives in. A system that has bread generations of people lacking some of the foundational skills needed to monetize their creativity and art. Well, we are not going to put up with this anymore. We are going to bring financial and business education to the group of people that need it, musicians.

In this book, you will not only learn the fundamental distinctions between art and business, but also how they work together and how we can avoid most of the fears and concerns people have about making more money or devoting enough time to their art.

We'll dive into the musicians who are "all about the money" and breakdown all the pitfalls that come with that line of thinking as well as give you a few examples of some musicians I've seen in my career fall prey to this trap and how you can avoid following in their paths. Unfortunately, the opposite perspective is not much better.

This is actuality a lot of more of a pervasive problem than the previous one, and that is the musicians who are strictly "all about the art". We'll dive into all the issues with ignoring your business and entrepreneurial side and still expecting to start to see progress or results in your music business.

On top of all that, you're also going to learn how to balance your art and your business. I do this by dividing what shifts we need to make into two categories: balancing art with business and balancing business with art. Now, while that may just sound like a meaningless turn-of-phrase, I use my words very carefully when making this distinction.

You as the musician, are in an interesting spot where 50% of what you're going to be focusing on is completely art-based. You'll be focusing on things like how the hook in the song should sound, what lyrics fit best, how more excitement can be introduced into a section, what key the song is going to be in, etc. Things like profit, lists, etc. are not even a consideration during the creative process. However on the other hand, you're going to be focusing the other 50% on enterprises that are almost strictly business in nature. You're going to be focusing on what kind of ads convert the best, which relationships you need to make to grow, how you're going to fund upcoming releases and videos, how you're going to put together a marketing campaign, etc.

When approaching these two seemingly contradicting tasks, you're going to have learn how to integrate very specific elements of your way of thinking as an artist into your thinking as someone in the music business. Those decisions will help you stay the course and not fall into traps I will list out in the "all about money" chapter.

This is also how you never turn-off fans when you give them opportunities to support you. On the flip side of the coin, whenever approaching your art, there are skills that you will learn from learning business that will help serve you in the areas of creating your art. This is how you look out for sharks in the water and also negotiate and maintain important relationships.

So if you're ready to learn how to balance these two forces and areas of your life, I'd like to welcome you to the Dilemma as well as the solution.

Now before we begin, I need to address some myths or false beliefs that exist out there in the culture of artists. I've seen these personally in my own career as well as heard stories from a lot of friends inside of the business. These four myths will broken down one by one, and by the end you will hopefully not have these internal roadblocks getting in the way of the true path of the music entrepreneur.

The 4 Harmful Myths That Perpetuate Failure

*"It ain't what you don't know that gets you into trouble.
It's what you know for sure that just ain't so."*
—*Mark Twain*

From the beginning of this business, the thing that has separated the people at the top from the people at the bottom has come down to two things: a knowledge gap and an action gap. The people who get results are simply not held down by false perceptions and stories that permeate our industry. These myths and false stories cause friction and hesitation. You will second guess good opportunities and miss out because of these myths.

The sad part is that these myths are considered common knowledge by a large percentage of artists who are trying to become professionals. These myths are sometimes passed down out of genuine ignorance to the truth, but sometimes these myths are perpetuated to keep artists in a dependent state and have to reply on people in the industry who are looking to take advantage of them. Famous entrepreneurial artist, Prince, once came out with the word "Slave" written on the side of his face in response to how he felt about Warner Brothers. Prince even disavowed his own name as a way to emancipate himself from the identify he had with Warner Bros. He went by a symbol for years to separate himself from Warner Bros.

Prince was an artist who figured it out early on. He understood that fundamentally the relationship between label and artist has always been a position of master and slave. There have been other artists before and after Prince who would discuss such situations inside the music business, but few went to the extent he did to pave his own path inside of an industry that had previously been built on dependence. Prince embodied someone who saw through all the bullshit. Sure, he was a very eccentric and quirky individual, but the way he saw to see the truth of this business ultimately led to a career where he was in charge.

This is the position I want you to be in. I want you to be the boss of your music business and your destiny inside this business. I want you to see through all the bullshit and be able to make smart choices so that you are not held down by false beliefs that lead to miscalculations, misinterpretations, and missed opportunities. The first myth that we'll break down is probably the oldest one you've heard in circles of musicians talking about some band that is having massive commercial success. The phrase "sold out" or "selling out" is usually tossed out there a few times, on top of a bunch of rationalizations as to why they aren't gatekeeping and their criticism is actually correct. It's "just the stupid masses" that make these artists popular and blah blah blah. These cynical conversations are older than you think and they actually come from a complete lack of understanding as to what those phrases actually mean or where they come from.

The next myth we'll bust will be one that has kept artists wasting their time doing activities that do not make a difference in their music businesses, and ultimately prevent them from making the progress they'd like in a timely manner. This myth is, I believe, a relic of a particular way of thinking is rooted in scarcity and pride. There is an old saying you've heard about that goes, "if you want something done right, you better do it yourself". People don't realize that this idea is fundamentally rooted in a lack of trust in other people and will ultimately lead to trouble in your relationships with your team members of your music business.

The third myth that we are going to be breaking down is one rooted in catchy sayings that we've heard from TV. Now, don't get me wrong, I love movies. My band and I quote movies incessantly in our van when we are traveling together. However, movies are full of a lot of bullshit that is passed off as wisdom. Movies have a way of using words and images to evoke certain thoughts and emotions regardless of the solidity of their truth claims. "If you build it, they will come" comes from a whisper to Kevin Costner in the movie "Field of Dreams". While this sounds like something that applies to real life, the reality is actually much different.

Finally, the last myth that we will be tackling will be one that I've seen cause a lot of hesitation among young artists or even artists who have been in this game for around 10 years and still refuse to learn. Self-sabotage is a real thing. People self-sabotage when they don't truly feel like they deserve the success they desire. Charlie Munger once said "to get what you want, you have to deserve what you want". That quote always stuck with me because it's not pretty but it's true. The world is not a crazy enough place to where they guy that eats junk food all day in excess will lose weight and put on muscle the way the guy in the gym eating healthy will. It's just not possible. In life we need to work to deserve the things in life that we desire. We also need to make room in our minds that we are worthy to achieve these goals. Otherwise we will forever be doomed to self-sabotage.

This final myth is a perfect example of self-sabotage. Certain artists believe that if they have success (aka loose their struggle that gave them something to write about) then they will lose their creative spark. In some way, necessity can help produce great pieces of art, but they are in no way the only way to do so. Artists sometimes find themselves having to create characters with pain that they can vicariously live through in the moment of writing a piece of music. The reality is that success comes from inspiration, and hardship is just one form of inspiration that can get the creative fires cooking. It just takes the humility to do something different that leads to an artist actually finding genuine creative inspiration. The rock artist finds a creative spark in diving into a genre that they are not used to. The rapper finds new creative spark when they find beats and grooves from other styles of music, and so on and so on.

Now, let's dive into each of these myths more in-depth so we can really break them!

Myth #1:
"Making Music For Success Is Selling-Out"

How many time have you seen an artist and thought to yourself, "wow, what a sell-out"? You see an artist who used to make music that was kind of underground, and only you and the small community that listened to them even knew they existed. Then they start to gather a bigger audience and their sound changes, and what does everyone think: "they just changed their sound to be more mainstream and sold out".

Maybe the artist has had a lot of success with one sound, but they change their sound to stay relevant, would you consider that selling out? What about a situation where a band loses a key member like a singer, and decided to take the band in a new direction with their new singer, would that be selling out?

There are bands who spend a good chunk of their time worrying about whether they are selling out, or trying to stick-it to the bands that have (in their minds) sold-out. All the while, their fanbases remain stagnant and money starts to dwindle, never thinking for once that they may be contributing to their lack of growth.

How many people have seen the show, Bar Rescue? Love it or hate it, the show is fascinating from the aspect of human psychology. You see people who start businesses that are essentially monuments to themselves and their ego, and when someone who could come in and help them gives them advice that will make the difference, what do they do?

They always freak out and even look at someone who has been in the business for 40 years and say things like "what do you know?" or "do you know anything about the bar business?"…seriously! Could you imagine a professional musician of 40 years who has had a lot of success you would like to see came up to you and gave you advice and you questioned their credentials the way this lady questions Jon's experience?

This is fundamentally how artists who are so stuck on "never deviating from 'who they are'", as if who they are is somehow defined by the culture of a niche or genre of music. How many times have you heard, "I'm a (insert genre) musician, I don't do that"?

As if modeling success is only limited to people who break the "rules" of their genre and therefore "sell-out", and they have more artistic integrity because they stayed within the box of what their genre allows. It is absolute nonsense and unhelpful.

The truth here is that the idea of "selling out" is a bunch of bull. If you go back and look at the history of that phrase, it actually has nothing to do with compromising your morals or your values. It actually has a meaning that reveals the true nature of the music business.

If you look back at the very first music business, it was publishing. I learned about this from pop artist Wil.I.Am. You had artists who wrote music, and therefore created a demand for people who performed the music or wanted to learn how to play these songs.

That means now there is demand for the sheet music, and once the sheet music is purchased, there will now be a demand for the instrument needed to perform the music. So you see how a whole economy can be built out of publishing music.

Out of the demand for the music came the demand for places to perform that music. Concert venues were born out of this demand and continue to provide this service to artists today. Now, where does selling out come to play with this?

Once phonographs and record players became a force of nature in introducing new music to a massive audience, including the introduction of radio, there were now ways music could be used to sell other things with it!

If you were on a station that played country songs, you might hear commercials in between songs for products like Levis jeans, Coors Light beer, or maybe even one for Ford F1-50. That's because the people purchasing those advertisement spaces know exactly who their audiences are.

Artists then started creating a huge demand to listen to the radio by creating the songs we know and love, or more accurately, that our grandparents know and love. However, since the US doesn't practice terrestrial radio rights, the artists never got to participate in the revenue generate by the playing of their songs on all these radio stations.

We can complain about this, but most of these artists were still able to make millions of dollars from their share of royalties from vinyls and eventual CDs. They still made a ton of money, but it shows you another business that is born out of music.

Okay, nice history lesson, but what does this have do with selling out? Well the original artists who were "sell-outs" were the people who sold outside of the things they were "supposed" to sell. Things like record players, vinyls, and phonographs were the main things that musicians were supposed to sell, as well as everything I mentioned about the publishing industry, the first music business.

They were writing jingles for commercials or appearing on commercials and selling things like Coca-Cola and Pepsi. Since these artists were using their name, and by proxy, their music to sell products that people felt were too commercial, they were labeled sell-outs.

They were labeled sell-outs not because they compromised their morals or values and starting change their art, but because they "broke the code", whatever that means, that they sold things they weren't supposed to sell.

Nowadays you have Dr. Dre using his music not sell other people's product's, but his own Beats by Dr. Dre, a product which has made him $3,000,000,000 dollars (87% of which is cash).

This is how musicians are supposed make their money. They're supposed to learn how to take their music and use it to sell their own products! You're literally doing what you're supposed to when you learn how to sell using your name or your music. Myth busted!

So now that you know that the idea of a "sell-out" is just a made up label created by envious industry players as well as artists, what do we do about it? The truth is you're going to have to find more than one way to make money from your music.

Don't let this shift in the game be what puts you on the sidelines, commit to making money from other avenues in your music business, including your music. It's not that you'll never make any money from your music, its that you're not reliant or dependent on your streaming sales.

There are plenty of merchandise items out there (I've even compiled lists of up to 107 different merch items to sell), and pretty much every musician has a good portion of their income coming from their merchandise sales.

Another valuable place you can make money is through live show tickets. If you're able to negotiate a descent door deal with a venue, and you bring a lot of fans, you can have a very profitable evening.

Pro tip: don't get too caught up in guarantees that are in the $100-$500 area, because if you bring enough people you can make 2-3x more money from a door deal with your local venue!

I remember one time my band KIRRA was playing a local show, and when we were booking it we had previously been getting guarantees of around $300-$400. This is something fairly difficult for an original band and we had worked really hard to build up enough of an audience to deserve that guarantee pay at the time.

So when the local venue owner said he would only be willing to book us under a door split, where you split the profits from the door sales, we were kind of pissed. This is something that venues only do for beginner local bands, right?

"Door splits? Are they serious? Does they have any idea how many shows we had to play to get OUT of playing for door splits? This is complete bull! We can bring plenty of people to this show! Does he not think we can bring people? What the hell!"

Nonetheless, we wanted to play our hometown because we had finally started to build up a following. We then set out to prepare for the performance and to start marketing the show, and that's when we had the awesome idea to have a VIP ticket! I'll talk more about this later in the book, but we showed up to the gig and loaded up gear and merch.

We had it in our minds that "okay, because we were getting paid from a door split we have to really make a lot of money on merchandise". This was from an out-dated experience with door splits.

When *we* were one of those amateur bands just starting out, we had experiences where we played headlining gigs when we shouldn't. From those gigs we had experiences where not many people showed up and therefore the door splits weren't great. However, we were able to sell a good chunk of the people that did show up and so our merch was our main source of income for a while. So from that we always assumed that you always want a guarantee because door splits never worked out well.

However, this was a big error on our part and in fact could've been recognized with a little math. If we could bring a lot of people, and we were making a percentage of every single person that walked through the door, then we could actually make a decent amount of money.

By the end of the night when it was all said and done, we had sold roughly $800 in merchandise, which was a pretty good night by our standards at the time. When I walked up to get the rest of the pay from our door split, I was dumbfounded that we had made a bit over $1,100 in money from the door split. On top of that, we had 7 people purchase VIP tickets which added another $250 or so to the total. Making it a roughly $3,150 night, and since we did well we decided to pay that $150 to one of our good friends who's band was performing as our direct support.

There are plenty of avenues that you can make money from as an artist that are outside of selling your music or just collecting streaming royalties.

Hopefully this has given you a start to where you can see that there are opportunities out there for you that you can achieve. I know being a professional musician can be a tough gig, but the rewards you get from setting yourself up properly and having success in your music business is totally worth the trials.

Don't let outside opinions of artists who are either too afraid, too lazy, or too cynical to go out there and take on the personal risk needed to actually have success in any business. There's never been any artist who had any long-lasting success that didn't take on risk in order to do so.

Putting yourself out there is a necessary part of becoming a professional, and sure, you might get haters. That doesn't mean that you aren't on to something great! Usually good art provokes people, and you need to make peace with that.

It will make sure that you don't get too wrapped up in superficial things which is what the *real* selling-out would be—to sacrifice your art for cheap, superficial trends or tricks.

"Myth #2:
If You Want Something Done Right, You Better Do It Yourself"

Before I completely rail on this saying, I understand there are certain circumstances where you should handle something yourself. Obvious examples like: writing your own music, performing your own music, or interacting with your audience.

There was a local band that were a young group of guys that just wanted to be a band, but they had only played covers at that point so writing new music was a bit of a challenge. Anyone who has ever tried to write a song certainly knows that it can be extremely difficult, and when you're a young group of guys that just want to start playing live sometimes you'll do anything to live the dream.

One of the members had a dad who started to write the bands lyrics, and it showed. It was bad. The lyrics were so bad and the dad was so controlling, that singers would come and go like crazy. I think they might have had 10 singers come and go through this band. Due to the fact that singers are a huge part of the brand of any group, this led to them having little success due to the fact that fans never knew what to expect. Sometimes the singers were good but the internal dynamics inevitably would force them out, or they were really bad singers that you could tell they were just using to be able to play shows.

I felt some sympathy for them for wanting to get out there, but having someone else create the message that you will ultimately be the face of is not the route you want to start going. You want to have a personal connection to the message because then you will fight for it!

However, the phrase you should be aware of is "highest and best use". Is going out and designing your own artwork the highest and best use of your time? Is managing your own tour the highest and best use of your time?

Yes, you could most certainly take care of these tasks yourself, and if you're starting out you'll definitely have to take care of that initially, but we all know that it is not the highest and best use of your time.

There's a wonderful book that changed my life called, "The 'E' Myth" by Michael Gerber. It talked about why most small businesses fail and the things that make a successful business work. This is definitely a must have for anyone who wants to get involved in any business, and as a musician, you're definitely a candidate.

One of the key takeaways from the book is that you need to structure your business in a way that you are working, as the owner, *on* the business as opposed to working *in* your business.

How many of you can relate to that? You spend so much time setting up your music business that you feel you're always behind because there is always something more to do and never enough time in the day to get it all done.

This is one of the biggest struggles ALL self-employed business owners have to deal with, and I don't want you to have to suffer anymore from this "if you want it done right, you have to do it yourself" trap.

The way out of this trap is to start setting up systems within your business to get things done. Now don't get me wrong, you will have to initially fill the role of the person who will eventually be fulfilling the system for you.

You want to go through the systems enough times to make sure the system even works in the first place. Then, once you have seen how the system works and know that it in fact works, you're ready to start replacing yourself.

I remember my band members and I would run our own merch (we still do, situation depending), but we ran it enough times not knowing what the heck we were doing as far as keeping all this inventory all straight at the same time you're selling to fans and trying to take pictures.

We did this for a long time, grinding night after night stumbling all over ourselves with the merchandise becoming increasingly disorganized as the tour goes on. Eventually, you get fed up with living in filth and you start to figure out more systems to make things easy to understand and easy to operate. Shout out to my wife who helped out a lot with the merch systems early on!

After years of accumulating a more and more refined merch table, it got to the point where we knew the moment we were ready to systemize. There was a show my band played while we were on tour with a national act in Nashville, TN. Nashville being a great music city, we knew we were in for a great night and also because it was a sold out show!

We ended up playing for about 1,300 people and as you can imagine with a crowd like that, you're going to be swamped at the merch table if you can pull off the right performance. Luckily for us, our singer Gabe had a friend who came in and offered to help run our merch.

While we typically don't let people behind the merch table that we just met, we had trust in Gabe's friend. It's not like she'd try to steal anything or something like that so we figured that there wasn't much harm to having someone run merch while we perform as well as before and after the show.

We took her back behind the merch table and started showing her the ropes of our systems. All the different tasks we do to mark how much is sold, what is sold, how to take credit card payments, and on and on. After about 2 minutes of going through all the different little parts of our systems, Stevie felt she could run the table and we believed in her.

So we went out there and played our hearts out to a sold out audience, and had probably one of our best nights on the whole run! We got off stage and half the band began to dive into "tear-down mode" and the other half began to head back stage to prepare to meet the fans at the merch table.

I grab some of the towels provided and the yellow gatorade (my personal favorite) and I opened up my Shopify app to check on credit card sales, and it was already at $541! Gabe and I headed out to the merch table to see a line and Stevie, someone who had just seen the systems that day for 2 minutes, running the merch stand like a pro.

This was the first time we had seen how impactful a set of systems and a great person can be when implemented in your business. Now, that's what happens when a great merch person is operating your systems. What happens if someone not so great operated it?

If you don't have systems that even the greenest newbie in the world could step in and smoothly operate, then your system sucks. Of course a system runs smoothly when a great person is running it, they're great! So I remember one of the band members family members who had a little bit too much to drink stepped in and started working the merch one night when no one was as the table.

Even someone who was intoxicated was running the system smoothly when I returned to the table as they were closing a sale with a fan. I was sold that we had built a great system and we were ready to hire someone to operate merch. This is a great lesson for all your systems inside your music business.

You should have a booking system that anyone could implement and get a show done, you should have a merch design system to have new designs always coming through your stores, etc.

After hearing how long it took us to get stuff together you might be thinking that building a business system is a super complicated and complex thing, but it's really super simple. In fact, I'm going to show you how to set up a business system right now!

All you have to do is outline exactly what tasks need to be done from the very beginning of the system's process, all the way to the very last tasks that wrap up whatever it is you're trying to accomplish.

You can do this very simply with a written step 1 through step 7 or however many you need until the task is completed and finalized.

Don't worry about being too literal with each step inside of your system. Systems are designed to be dummy proof, meaning it's so simple to complete that literally anyone of any education and background could complete these tasks.

Think about McDonalds for a moment. While I won't comment on the quality of their food because I think we all know what we are paying for when you order from McDonalds. You're definitely paying for convenience more than you are paying for quality.

However, when it comes to the business systems of McDonalds, they have some of the best in the world. One of the signs a business has their systems dialed in is when you have franchise opportunities for that business.

The story of how Ray Kroc took McDonalds from a tiny burger stand into a billion-dollar company is an interesting one. If you've seen the movie "The Founder" you might think Ray Kroc is a bad guy. However, what they don't tell you is that Ray never took a dime for a paycheck for the first 8 years he was involved with McDonalds.

I want you to imagine that, you never take a dime for a paycheck for 8 years, but you know you're working towards something greater so you keep going. You know there is something there and you now must see it out to the end.

Well it all payed-off one day when he discovered he could make more money from owning the land underneath the buildings that were McDonalds than he would with a royalty agreement to make 15% off 20 cent hamburgers. Does this situation feel familiar? Getting paid pennies for something that takes a lot of work and time to build?

Ray's story can be found in a book called "Grinding It Out" that I would recommend you check out. He turned a burger business into a full blown real estate empire accompanied by a franchised business that runs completely on systems. Your business will also need to eventually run a lot on systems.

A franchise is a sign of a turn-key business that anyone could purchase from you and operations would have no change in procedure. Now while you're probably not planning on selling your business to someone else as an artist, you might be preparing to expand your operations with a record label or distribution company.

Having systems in place that someone who is investing in you can accentuate will make investing in you seem like a more attractive idea. That's because there is no set up cost for them, they can just throw money at an already converting system that you have set up.

Typically when artists get involved with record labels, there is this terrible expectation that the label will do the work of building the artists audience for them and all they will have to do is worry about creating art.

However, this is very seldom the reality of the situation. Usually what happens is even if you have success with a record label, you don't own anything even though it's your music and your brand.

All of these troubles that an artist can find themselves in comes from properly rejecting the "if you want something done right, do it yourself" attitude, but failing to discern on where to apply this more delegating-style of approach.

You do not, and I repeat, <u>DO NOT</u> outsource the task of building your own audience! That is something for you to do and if you put this on someone else, you will most likely lose any control or ownership or your work.

I remember seeing a TikTok where a young female artist was complaining because she felt that it was the responsibility of labels to get an artist discovered by a wider audience, and it was the responsibility of the artists to write great music.

Hey, if you want to go back to time where the artists were basically slaves to the labels and had little-to-no control over their music or little-to-no ownership of their music, then there are predators in this business that are waiting idly by to promise you the world for a pretty hefty price tag.

You should outsource something like designing your next t-shirt for your merchandise. I know there will inevitably be some people who are skilled in graphic design or art that will suggest they're better off creating their artwork than someone else, which is fine.

I do know, however, that there are other tasks like booking a tour that every musician should strive to delegate regardless of their other artistic skills, or running the ship while out on the road by being a tour manager.

Learning how to systemize your music business will be one of the keys in giving you more time and more opportunities to grow and expand your reach as well as your income.

Don't fall prey to the myth that you have to be the one doing everything because you can't trust that anyone can do anything as good as you. I know that sounds kind of harsh, but fundamentally distrust is where this saying comes from.

Instead of questioning someones own judgement in delegating the proper person to fulfill a task, they would rather say that "people are dumb, and if you want something done right, you better do it yourself".

Have more faith in people because there are good booking agents, and there are bad booking agents. There are good promoters, and there are bad promoters. There are good tour managers and bad tour managers.

Take responsibility for not finding the right people if you have not already. Taking extreme ownership of your life is how you're going to see any real change. Now go and start building systems so you can fill those roles with other good people who are up to the task.

"Myth #3:
If You Build It, They Will Come"

How many times have you heard this one? You're told to just build it, and then the fans will come, just start a band and the fans will come, just play shows and the fans will come. I was even told this as advice by the singer of one of my favorite bands.

It was right after the first time I ever saw them, and I was blown away by the intense live show I had just seen. Then I saw that the lead singer was hanging out over by the merch booth and I knew I wanted to meet this person and ask advice on how to get where they were!

I ran through the hundreds of people that were at this sold-out show and finally got to him. I told how much I enjoyed the show and asked him "if you could give advice to your younger self starting out knowing everything you know now, what would you say?"

I had kind of put him on the spot a little bit, and after thinking for a second or two, he said "I'm not sure man, maybe if you build it they will come", and he told me that really he meant it like: "just keep going, never quit".

However, why does this phrase keep coming back and does it actually work to just build it and they will start showing up and supporting you? Well, I took that singers advice to heart and never gave up, but in the beginning stages I was doing a whole lot of building and was disheartened to not see a lot of people showing up.

I can tell you that I implemented that strategy for the first 3 years of my bands career and it did not do very much for us. In fact, it really didn't do anything. You can't just expect people to (in todays world) just go on an in-depth search to find you when people are surrounded by so many options.

In fact according to Spotify's Loud & Clear site, nearly 80% (78.4%) of artists on Spotify today – around 6.3 million of them – have a monthly audience on the platform *smaller* than 50 people.

This is one of the downsides of the information age, which is that we are inundated with a near infinite number of musical options and getting your music to stand out amongst the sea of other bands is not something you can nor should leave up to chance.

Which is exactly what you're doing when you just build it and just expect them to come. You're relying on the chance that the algorithm will show your music as opposed to other artists who are in fact taking an effort to get their name known.

The music business is competitive and if you're not willing to get out there and start to market yourself with confidence, then you're going to have a very rough time in this business. I hope you take this as motivation to get off the sidelines and get in the game, there is plenty to go around!

There will always be room for new artists trying to make a name out there as long as you have something that is compelling enough to move people and get them to have a positive experience with your art.

A lot of people have great art but they have no methods or strategies to get their name out there or to create any buzz or awareness about them or their upcoming releases. This is the bane of all musicians lives. It doesn't mean that you have to all of a sudden care about what other people think, or that you have to be obsessed with how many followers you have.

What this means is that it's time that you start getting intentional about your marketing and start figuring out exactly who you want to serve. I know most musicians are thinking to themselves, "I want everyone to like my music", and while we certainly want as many people to listen to our music as possible, we need a core audience that we are going to build a career from.

It's similar to the thousand fan theory where you need a core, die hard audience that will support you and give you the financial stability to have a career in music. Its from this position, that you can start expanding your reach to a more wide-spread audience and have more omnipresence online.

When I very first switched from being an employee to an entrepreneur, I needed a secure financial foundation upon which I could then start to focus on my music business enough to get results I wanted, and this is a big analogy to being a professional musician. I remember when I had the idea, I was stuck in this weird dilemma because I had been at this job for 3 years and met some great people, but I knew my dream was to be a music entrepreneur or professional musician.

Before I could get there, I needed to free myself from the 9-5 cycle of punching in and punching out for someone else. I decided to focus on the easiest shift I could make to free myself because if it was too hard to switch, I would probably take longer to make it happen. I was a music instructor for a big music corporation, and so why not just become a private music instructor where I am my own boss?

To do that, I needed to figure out how many students I need to make the same amount of money I was making at that big music corporation. I had around 25 students at the time with this company, and I found out I only needed 8 to quit my job. Literally only one third of the previous amount of students I had were needed.

The best part was that I would be making the same, if not a bit more, amount of money, and I would only spend 7 hours a week as opposed to 25 hours plus my 20 mile commute. That's a fifth of the time I was previously spending on my money making activities! Imagine if you cut your jobs hours down to a fifth of what they were but you were making the same money. If you knew that was possible, would you do it?

If you're wondering if I'm just bragging or if I have a point, let me ask you a question. Do you have a better chance to become a professional musician if you have to slave away at a job you hate that takes a majority of your time and energy or if you're the boss of your own side business that allows you to focus more time and energy on your dreams?

I would be willing to bet the second option would be your best bet at having a life that doesn't feel so consumed by the rat race, and the other is going to throw so many restrictions on how you can make your dreams happen that it puts you at a major disadvantage to everyone who has figured this out. Your main tasks are to get more time & more money to invest into your music business. When you have a job, your dreams and your music career are in the hands of your manager, supervisor, or whomever makes the decisions in that business.

I remember when a local act had to find a new bass player for a tour because their original bassist's job said he couldn't go on tour. That sucks doesn't it? You're trying to make your dreams happen and get to work on something productive, and your job says "no". You had no say-so, there was no compromise, you were just forced to eat the decision that negatively effected your music business and there was nothing you could do about it.

Jobs for artists provide a false sense of security. Even when you have a great job as an artist that provides you benefits, you could lose that job tomorrow, have people promoted over you, or hell even if they go out of business. It's all secure, until it's not. We want security but you want "freedom-based" security, as apposed to "scarcity-based" security. Freedom-based security means you have financial security but you also have more freedom to make unanimous decisions to improve your business. Where as scarcity-based security is the idea that you have security but only just enough, and you're not in control so really it could be gone any minute.

The main point is that you need to act from a position of freedom-based security. Focus on building the first 1,000 fans you'll need to have the support you need to take more risks to expand. It's tougher to take risks that might actually pay off if you don't have security to fall back on, and if you have more time to invest, you can actually ensure that nothing is half-assed.

So you've got to figure out who your core audience is so that you can start to not just build, but attract that audience so they will come check out whatever you've got going on. A lot of this comes down to branding, but it also has to do with your style of music.

For instance, if you're a dreamy, dark style of pop music then maybe you want to target Billie Ellish's audience for your next music video release! That way the audience you're sending your music too is already primed to enjoy your sound.

Another example would be if you have a more classic thrash metal type sound, then maybe you should send your advertisements to Metallica's audience. It wouldn't make sense to send it to Taylor Swift's audience since they would probably hate what you're presenting them.

Hey who knows, there might be a small percentage of Taylor Swift's audience that is diverse enough in their listening habits to also like you, but is it worth spending money on advertisement to that audience when you could get a lot more specific with your targeting, probably not.

Either way, don't let the comfort of staying where you are and doing the things you are most conformable doing keep you stuck. If you want to start making positive changes in your life your going to have to do things that are probably new for you.

Like they say, there's no change without a change in routine. If you're doing the same things you've always done, expect to get the same results you've always gotten.

You might be thinking those are just cliches, but I can tell you first hand there is a lot of wisdom in those words and there is a reason people repeated them in the first place. Never forget why something became a cliche in the first place.

It might just reveal whether you're dealing with a genuine piece of wisdom that will help you or just Hallmark empty sayings. I want to tell you a story where I wanted to have more time to focus on my business, so back when my wife, then-girlfriend and I were hanging out we'd hang out all night when we were first dating. We would hang out as soon as we could, often having lunch together. Then we would just go to the mall or something just to mess around or go play video games at my house. We would play games like Left 4 Dead and then just snack and watch movies all night long.

I'd take her home around 2 or 3 in the morning sometimes, and as you could imagine, when I got home there wasn't really anytime to focus on my business. So instead of saying "I just don't have time for that", I started to, unbeknownst to my wife (then-girlfriend), creating a curfew where I would take her home around midnight, so that the rest of the night could be focused on my business.

After changing that habit, I started to actually make progress because I had the time to devote to it. A lot of people think about changing habits and starting new productive habits, but a lot also stop at thinking and don't actually start making changes. Some people feel strange limiting time with their significant other so that they can pursue their dreams, but that's the sacrifices you will inevitably have to make.

I needed to spent that time away so I could go create a situation where I was making enough and because of that I actually had more time to spend with her. This is setting yourself up for the long haul as opposed to making decisions purely in the present.

When you change the behavior, you change the outcome. If you don't change the behavior you'll never get a different outcome. It's time to start finding areas of your day that you can start carving out for your future because only then will you start to change the outcomes you've been running into.

I remember when I used to play a lot of video games. I would spend all day playing games with my friends and then we would play late into the night and early morning. I had always played video games from my youth, but I really didn't get the social gaming experience until I got Call of Duty 4. My family and friends would start clans and play together all the time. It became a pretty normal part of daily life, until I was about 18.

I had just finished beating Assassin's Creed: Brotherhood, after beating the first and second Assassin's Creed. As you can imagine, I spent a lot of time on those games exploring the huge worlds that are in those games. I had the next two games, Assassin's Creed: Revelations & III, lined up after I had beat Brotherhood. I put in the disc for Revelations, and as I began the gameplay I had a thought, "what am I really accomplishing by beating this?". I knew I was at the beginning of investing another large set of hours to complete and master this game.

What was I actually going to have to show for it, or for all the hours I spent on all the other games I had been playing? The only thing close to a real accomplishment was when I got 36th in total points in the world on drums inside Guitar Hero: Metallica. It was a little nerdy flex I had, and the girls I were trying to go out with did not find it as much of a flex.

It was that moment, looking at my character in the game just standing on a snowy castle-side that I decided to turn the game off and give up video games recreationally. Since I did that, I had so much more time to improve my life. I had time to hone in my skills on my instrument, I had time to dedicate to learning business, I had time to write more for my band.

It was an all around great decision to put down the controller. I couldn't be distracted for my entire 20's, I knew that couldn't be the way forward. How many people have wasted their 20's because they were still acting they were 18? How many music careers could've been started in that time that never did because the artists were too distracted conquering imaginary worlds that they never had time to work on the one real life they have.

This one life we have is precious and the time we have here is valuable. Do not squander this valuable time to goof off and do what is easiest, but use this time to get leverage on all the people who are still wasting their time. This is the easiest time in the world to have success because there are so little competition that is actually hungry and willing to commit and go for it.

If you can start changing the behaviors that are keeping you back, you can begin to start changing the outcome you're currently experiencing in your music business. Beware though, as Warren Buffett once said, "the chains of habit are often too weak to be felt until they're too strong to be broken".

Are you feeling ready to start publishing and putting your music and videos out for the world to see? I hope so! This is how you can overcome the rut of just believing "if you build it, they will come". Time to start taking control of your destiny and getting yourself known!

"Myth #4:
Success Will Hurt My Creativity"

This is probably the worst myth, and it's one of the reasons I saved it for last. There have often been so many toxic narratives about business and how if you provide value for people and manage to make a buck that somehow you're a bad person.

Can you name a film in the last 50 years that positions the guy making money as the good guy? Did you have to go to Google or IMDB to find the answer? I certainly had to. I know it took me a while before I could even have an answer.

Before I point this out, know that I'm not trying to be a stick in the mud, I actually enjoy most of these films. I know there are other lessons inside of most of these films, but the clearly one-sided way of viewing the world is pretty apparent once you see the connecting themes.

-In "The Social Network", Mark Zuckerberg, who for all his flaws is the guy who perfected the social networking site as we know it, is positioned as the bad guy who's ego got too big and screwed over his friend and got taken advantage of by the even worse guy, Sean Parker.

-In "Office Space", the only way three friends who hate their corporate job can seem to muster to create a new life for themselves is to commit fraud to steal "pennies" from the company they're quitting or getting fired from. Well it turns out they steal the money and get away with it since one of the other disgruntled employees burned the building down. (They should've given him his stapler...)

-In "Fight Club", we see the insomniac protagonist (whether the director or author meant it to or not) positioned as the "hero" for bringing down the credit buildings with records that underlies most individuals and businesses balance sheets, causing total financial chaos. Yup, that's the good guy, but at least we had that cool twist though I guess?

-In "The Founder", Ray Kroc has a pretty amazing story (I'll mention more about it later), and its a great story for music entrepreneurs. Ray worked hard for a long time, 52 years in fact of his life, until he got his break when he came across the first McDonalds in San Bernardino. Ray is not positioned as some entrepreneurial hero in the movie, but more of a shady salesmen who saw that the McDonald brothers had a great system and as a result a great burger. Then decided to screw them out of money by starting a real estate business without the McDonald brothers, the guys who came up the idea. Really makes you want to be an entrepreneur right? Not.

-In "Wall Street", Gordon Gecko's iconic line "greed is good", was taken by a whole generation of young entrepreneurs as a green light to be negligent and reckless with greed, as evidence by another film "The Wolf of Wall Street" where even though Jordan Belfort has stated publicly how much he regrets his actions, it doesn't make the movie any less glamorizing of that behavior. For some artists, this may be enticing, but for a lot of other artists its repelling to the idea of being an entrepreneur.

Considering these movies and more, there have been many different moves in popular culture to demonize someone who attempts to go out and make something of themselves. However, you will not fall prey to the moral predators that are out there, not if you can learn the ways of real entrepreneurship.

The fact of the matter is that you can make a profit from your music business without hurting your relationship with your art. In fact, the most recent shift in the music business towards streaming has realigned the incentives of artists forever.

Let me explain, if there is an economic incentive to make music then there will be people who make music solely for that economic incentive. However if there is little to no economic incentive to create music, then the only people who will want to make music are the people who genuinely love music.

Imagine a situation where artists have the power to sell tickets directly to their fans, bypassing scalpers ability to buy them up and resell them at an inflated price. Imagine a situation where ordinary artists are making steady monthly income from their fan clubs and merchandise.

Now, I know that is not exactly the current scenario we live in, but it's getting close. It is where the incentives have shifted though, and once artists take their place in history where we became self-reliant. No longer beholden to 3rd parties within the music industry that have parasitized our economic value for too long.

We've had record labels owned by huge conglomerates centralize the output of mainstream music for basically a century, and that was disrupted with the introduction of streaming technology and I think ultimately blockchain will also help alleviate artists as well from this centralized control.

If there is any business that is harmful to your creativity, it's that. Having no control or ownership over your music, yet being beholden to a contract that has you basically in a debt-trap designed to keep you under control by the labels to keep pumping out profit for them.

I am kind of picking on labels a bit here, but I'm mostly referring to the big guys and the sharks who prey on the little guy. There is believe or not a middle ground of labels who actually care about their artists and want to provide fair deals, I've worked with one.

Outside of the scope of labels, there is however, a great music business where the artist is providing direct value to fans and get funding directly from fans & businesses via the offers and products that you give your fans. That is ultimately where you want to be.

Have you noticed all of this has nothing to do with how you write your songs? The only people who could have ever in a million years effect your songwriting are record labels that have a vested interest in changing your song to match a sellable sound.

Now that they have less of importance in how artists build an audience, they have taken a more venture capital position in the music industry. Which is fine, let artists who have business systems and fans built work with labels. We will make plenty of money on our own.

You see that we don't have to worry about business effecting our creativity because the very fact we are now in charge of our own business will require creativity of its own! It's all in the same domain as the creativity you use when you're thinking of a cool way to improve your live show, or think of a concept for your next music video.

I remember one time when I was working on some music with my singer Gabe who is one of the most creative people I know, and he told me that he had a great idea for a music video but he didn't know what song it would go with or how we would be able to pull it off. He told me of an idea where a female aerialist is twirling in the air as we're playing, but we would be set up in a circle around her. The room would be dark and slightly lit by spotlight or lamplight.

After hearing these ideas I was sold on the idea, but not sold how we were going to be able to pull something like that off with the budget we had at the time. So we kind of dropped the idea for a while until we had a single we had just written that we thought would actually be a perfect fit for this video idea.

On top of that, he had the idea because the song was titled "Flesh Gives Way" that we would actually start to look more physically wounded as the song went on. You know...like our flesh was giving way? Super clever I know. (lol!)

Plus, we knew that if we put the idea off any further that it just might not happen because it doesn't fit with the next song and so we can't go back and re-shoot a video for a single that would be 3-singles old. We had to act now if we had any chance of making this happen.

We went into crazy research to try and find the crew we needed to pull this off. First were the photographers for the behind the scenes footage, but also a make-up artist who would apply the different special effects make-up we needed. Luckily we knew a photographer, Chris, from our previous shoots, and Gabe's girlfriend at the time, Elyse, who could do the special effects makeup.

We still needed to figure out who was going to shoot this, who was going to be our aerialist, and where we were going to shoot this dang thing! Again, Gabe being a resourceful music entrepreneur, reached out to one of his long time friends, Jessica, who knew exactly how to pull off the stunts we were needing. She in fact was a music entrepreneur as well by creating and selling her art pieces as well as these performative acts.

Then out of nowhere, while Gabe was doing his 9-5 which at the time was being a furniture delivery driver and builder, he ran into a gentleman by the name of Reagan, who proceeded to tell Gabe he runs a videography company that has worked with bands before.

Reagan is a A-player, and when you find A-players, you pay them what they're worth. However, we had to find $4,000 of funding to make this deal happen. We negotiated with some investors taking on half of the music video fee, so we reduced it down to $2,000. Luckily for us we had just gotten done playing a bunch of shows and saving a bunch of money as a consequence.

It was one thing after another going in our favor, until it came time to find a location. Finding a location that is wide enough to house a full four-piece band but also tall enough to have an aerialist perform safely and at the height we needed for the shot, was a pain in the neck to say the least.

We tried theaters, but they were too expensive. We tried dance studios, but they were too short. We tried aerialist studios but they were too narrow. We tried gyms for gymnasts, but they were booked solid. It felt like everywhere we could try to find somewhere that had the height we needed as well as something that could safely suspend Jessica in the air seemed to be like an impossible task.

Finally, Reagan found a contact for a schools basketball gym in Chickasha, OK. We couldn't believe it, we were all set to shoot this video. We had the idea, we got the crew, and we now had the location. A feeling of relaxation came over me as I now realized the only thing we had to do now was do what we do best, play our music and perform to the best of our abilities.

We showed up, did our thing from two o'clock in the afternoon to two o'clock at night, Jessica showed up and worked from about seven o'clock to two o'clock, and we were wrapped. The crew was so excited over pushing through all odds to make this video happen, and working with people that made what could have been a very painful process into something that was fun and ended up being probably our best music video up to that point (until the next one).

Do you see how Gabe's creativity and resourcefulness played a pivotal role in making sure that this video could happen? This is the big lesson I want you to learn from this story. You must be resourceful, and being resourceful is a matter of creativity and focus. You as a musician are full of creativity!

Creative people are just that, creative! It only makes sense that the skills that serve you as a musician will serve you in your business.

Business isn't some rigid world of black and whites, it's just as much a creative venture as anything you do in the creation of music. We've been conditioned in a way to believe business is boring and complex so we should let some "professionals" take care of it for us before we even know what it would even look like.

You are completely capable of taking care of any of the business that will be required of you. The only time you may have an issue is if you're unbalanced with your art and your business, and that's what we are going to be talking about in the remainder of this book.

Now that I have hopefully debunked or broken down each of these myths that would be holding you back, I think you're ready to dive into how to balance your art and your business. We'll be going all the way from the most unbalanced perspectives to how we can start finding balance and have a peaceful balance between our music and our business.

Let's recap, you've learned that the whole idea that someone is a sell-out is a mostly made up term for people who were mad artists were making more money than them, and it is in no way a statement of you compromising your morals or your art.

You've learned that one of the common pieces of wisdom we've been told is actually slowing down our progress. We've learned that trust is key in building anything worth a value and we should always be doing something that is our highest and best use your time.

Another thing you've learned is that just because you build it, does not mean that people will just start showing up. Because of that fact, we are going to have to be brave and start publishing more so people can start to find out who we are.

Also you can target specific audiences that will be most receptive to your sound that way you can start reaching the fans that will be your core support throughout your career.

Finally, we've tackled the myth of business effecting creativity in a negative way, as if the two were oil and water. You've learned that actually couldn't be farther from the truth, and that business is just as much a creative activity as creating music is.

Throughout the remainder of this book you will also find challenges to common narratives about what it means to be a professional musician. I needed to knock out the most pervasive myths in the beginning, but there are still plenty more things that need to be challenged.

I hope you're now ready to dive into the musician's dilemma with no false preconceptions of the music business or what it means to be a professional musician. You have one of the most important gifts that has the power to really help make life better.

Fredrick Nietzsche once said, 'without music, life would be a mistake".

Being Unbalanced

*"There's no risk when you go after a dream. There's a
tremendous amount to risk when playing it safe."*
—Bill Burr

Counter-intuitively to the message I've given you so far, I want to make a weird clarification when it comes to being "unbalanced". There is a healthy "unbalance" and an unhealthy "unbalance" whenever it comes down to anything in your life. I know, it sounds a little confusing right?

An "unhealthy" unbalance would look something like spending all your money on DLC for video games when you could be investing that money into your skills and your knowledge. It could even be spending all your time looking up music theory concepts when you should be writing. It could be spending all your money on gear you don't need when you should be investing in promotion for your most recent release.

A "healthy" unbalance would look something like spending two days shooting batches of content for your social media. It could be diving into a 8 hour writing session with your band and writing mates. It could even be taking a few days to rehearse your setlist for a tour. All of these things would be things that will actually give you some progress. Whereas the "unhealthy" unbalance would definitely take up your time but on top of that, not give you any progress in your music career.

This is an important distinction to make because it will set up this entire section and give you the proper way to view this concept of being unbalanced. I don't want anyone avoiding great opportunities because they would require a bit of unbalance in your life. I remember when my wife and I were dating, and in the year 2016, I played around 145 shows. It definitely effected our relationship at times, but because I was able to go and capitalize on that opportunity, I ended up building relationships, lessons and systems, that I use to this day.

I'll tell you one of the most important things I learned about myself from studying personality psychology, which is that I am high in something called "neuroticism". Which is basically a fancy word for negative emotion.

There was a Forbes article that mentioned that people who are high in neuroticism are high in creativity. Now that doesn't mean that just because you're creative that you're a negative person, but if you find yourself struggling with negative thinking then maybe you can relate.

You can split neuroticism into 2 sub-categories: volatility and withdraw. Volatility means you're up and down all the time, like the stock market. Withdraw means you'll easily retreat when faced with conflict, whether that be literally leaving to distract yourself or just locking up emotionally.

Well, I'm very high in both of these categories, 90th percentile to be exact. Which means out of 100 people, I'm more neurotic than about 90 of them. Now, what could I have done with that information once I learned it?

I could've let that consume my world and just laid down and told myself some stories that would've kept me exactly where I was, or I could've realized that those are where my personality's pitfalls are and try to be conscious of when I start to act too volatile or too withdrawn.

If you're curious I went with the latter, and from doing that, I started to see where I was making mistakes in my life based off being too withdrawn or too volatile. This allowed me to form better bonds with the people I cared about most in my life. If you're readying this, I'm sure there is at least one person in your life who you would like a better relationship with.

Once you understand how personality types works you'll be able to see not only your own psychological pitfalls, but those of the people around you. Hopefully knowing what you know, you will have a bit more patience with people as well as a bit more empathy, because everyone has there own pitfalls they're dealing with and working on just like you and I are.

One of the first things you need to understand to become more balanced, is your own personality. Being a musician, there is a very high likelihood that your personality is geared more towards the creative and abstract, and with that comes a bunch of pitfalls: a proclivity to be very bad at forming schedules and sticking to them.

Becoming easily distracted and trying to do 100 things on the way to doing the 1 big task we had for that day. Getting easily caught up in what *might* happen as opposed to forming a plan to deal with those type of things. These are not universal statements of fact but propensities that people who exude certain personality traits will have to deal with at some point in their lives.

For a bit more clarification, I'm using a reference to something called "The Big 5 Model" which is a psychological model of personality types and the character traits. Individuals who fit certain personality types will on average have certain proclivities towards specific behaviors. It's important to recognize where your personality types are so you can see your strengths and your weaknesses. It's a true old saying that says the first step in fixing a problem is to acknowledge it.

You may think it's a cliche, but you have to consider why it was used to the point of a becoming cliche. It's because there is so much truth to it that it's pretty much a universal statement. There are a few different personality tests you can take online. I'd recommend a Big 5-based personality test or the Hexaco Personality Test (which in my estimation has just been an attempt to expand upon the Big 5 Model).

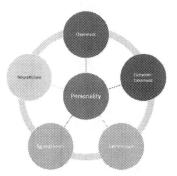

Learn where you shine and learn where your weaknesses are. Once you identify which of your personality types are in higher percentiles or lower percentiles, you want to start to notice when your less productive personality traits start to make themselves known.

For instance, if you're lower in "politeness" (one of the two subsets of agreeableness), you will probably be more blunt than most people and not notice when you're being a bit aggressive with your opinions. If that's the case, be on the look out for your tone of voice when being passionate about ideas and try not to be dismissive.

If you're high in "compassion" and "politeness" by contrast, you will have the proclivity to put others needs before yourselves. This will make it easier for people to walk all over you if you're not mindful of when you're being too agreeable.

In the music business, this could be catastrophic to negotiating favorable terms for your record contracts, publishing deals, or show terms. So wherever your personality is "lacking" in certain areas, don't have a fixed mindset or be deterministic. Find out ways that you can integrate that side of your personality in a healthy way, without this conscious effort, a lot of these patterns of behavior will happen unconsciously.

I remember when I saw an amazing drummer named Thomas Lang describe his process for eliminating problems in his drum playing that I thought was not only a genius way of looking at practicing a musical instrument, but also has a great analogy into your mindset. He writes down all of his weaknesses on a piece of paper, and slowly but surely he works on each weakness one at a time and once he has mastered one weakness, he moves on to the next. Until as he says, "then eventually I have no more weaknesses".

Now, there will never be a time unfortunately where we have removed all of the weaknesses of our character. There will always be a devil on one shoulder and an angel on the other, the two wolves, or however you want to symbolize this struggle. However, if we can identify which weaknesses are causing us the most distress and trouble in our lives, we can start to get control over those weaknesses as opposed to being subjected to them.

You may not be able to always get rid of negative thoughts, but you need to know how to deal with negative thoughts and not let them control you.

I have to talk about this next topic because it's one of the biggest sources of unbalance in peoples lives, and if not properly treated and maintained it can make even the best moments seem horrible. I'm talking about relationships. Now, if you're single, there is still something you can learn so when the day comes that you want to find someone to settle down with, it will help.

Lastly, spouses and significant others are often blamed by musicians as the reason they never pull the trigger on their dreams, and I need you not to do this. Do not use someone you care about as an excuse not to take action on your dreams.

Some musicians seem to think that becoming a professional musician means quitting their job immediately and doing nothing but hitting the road and only making money from your music ventures forever. That is not practical, common, or a valid excuse to use as a response to why someone hasn't committed to their dreams. It typically goes like this:

Person #1: Yeah, if I didn't already have descent career, or if I didn't have a family depending on my steady income, I would quit and pursue my passion to have a music career.

Person #2: Well there's actually no rule that says you have to quit your job immediately to be a professional musician. You can start by making extra money in a side hustle and put your music business systems in place in your free-time.

Person #1: Oh, but I'd have to tour eventually right? I don't think my wife would be down with that.

Person #2: Not necessarily, there are tons of ways to monetize music without having to tour. Some bands have put together online-only projects that have never played a live show ever and make good money from their online sales.

Person #1: Yeah, but how will I have time? Don't people who have side hustles have no time?

Person #2: Quite the opposite. My first side hustle took my workload from 30 hours a week to 6 and a half hours and I make the same money

I did at my old job. I have way more time to focus on my music business than before!

Most of the excuses or objections people put in their own way aren't really there most of the time. An old Roman philosopher named Seneca once said, "we often suffer more in imagination than in reality". I want you to be able to maintain stability in your relationships, but I don't want you to use your comfort zone as an excuse to start blaming other people for not taking action on your dreams.

Also If you're in a relationship, you might want to have your significant other take the previously mentioned personality tests. This will allow both of you to see each others results and try to work to understand when both of you are starting to become dominated by one side of their personality, and work to understand and help each other become the best versions of yourselves.

This is something that you must do with great care and empathy. Do not use this information was ammunition against your partner in arguments, that is not a healthy way to view each other in a relationship. This is information to help you both grow and not let your individual peculiarities interfere with the life you both want.

Last thing on relationships, this may sound like a cliche, but you must have excellent communication. If you do not communicate what is expected of each other, you will be constantly frustrated by not being on the same page.

My wife and I, for instance, have weeks of the year where tours are off-limits. This unfortunately came from some trial and error which resulted in some fights and missed occasions, but you don't have to make the same mistakes I did. Once we established this boundary, I put it into my bands system and we've never had that fight ever again.

My wife and I have a lot of personal events that happen in November and December. There are birthdays, holidays, anniversaries and all kinds of different things. One time a tour opportunity came across our desk and when we saw that we were getting to play with a band that had a pretty nice following and they were cool guys, we just impulsively said yes.

I remember coming home and I was so excited because this was a great opportunity to end a very productive year for my band. I got home, I parked the car, and walked in to my wife cooking dinner. She makes the best food and she was making homemade turkey burgers which are one of my favorite dinners she makes.

I walked and with a huge grin on my face said "hey honey, we got a big tour opportunity!", and because my wife has always been very supportive she responded, "that's great, babe! When is it?". I replied, "November!".

That's when her enthusiastic smile turned into a very hurt frown, and it hit me like a thousand tons of bricks...I had totally messed up. I couldn't believe I had totally forgotten all my personal obligations and didn't even talk to my wife before confirming something like that. From then on, I decided I needed to figure out what months were off limits and always talk with my wife about big tours that might be around important dates.

It literally made our relationship stronger by giving us both a sense of certainty and significance for each other. We felt certainty by reassuring that I would always be home for the most important moments of the year, and significance by demonstrating that we can both sacrifice for each other. I don't take tour opportunities in those weeks no matter how good the opportunity, and she doesn't mind me touring as much as I want in return.

Learn to communicate what you both need from each other so that you can both live your fullest lives. I see tons of musicians that have fears about what will happen to their relationship if they were too seriously committed to their music career. I wanted to at least help get some progress going.

Okay, that's enough psychology for now. What I want to dive into next are the two one-sided ways most musicians treat their business, and that's being "all about the money" and "all about the art". Remember this image from before?

"All About The Art"   **"All About The Money"**

Being all about the money is something you usually see from road-worn professionals after not optimizing their business inside the music industry or from superstars who have lost connection with their roots and why they do what they do. You may also see it from the over zealous up and comers who think they can cheat the system by doing all the superficial things necessary to satisfy the industry powers that be. They don't really care if their music isn't really "theirs" anymore. They want the lifestyle of the big famous artist who roles around in a lambo and has all the shiny luxuries artists can desire. They may think things like: "who cares about who owns the songs and if I'm a label puppet now, I have a fancy house and lots of cars". This is unsustainable for obvious reasons, but none-the-less a lot of musicians find a way to push themselves in this position.

"All About The Money"
Progress
Consistent
Avoid Pain
Convention
Profit
Certainty
Demographics

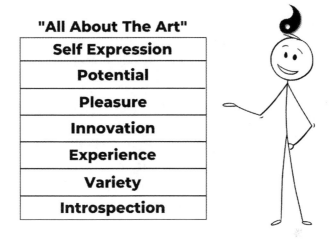

"All About The Art"

Self Expression
Potential
Pleasure
Innovation
Experience
Variety
Introspection

The other side is being all about the art, which most musicians consider not to be a negative at all, and on the surface and in moderation there is nothing wrong with it. However, when trying to become a professional musician there are inevitably things you will have to learn that are typically considered boring to you, and when you're "all about the art" it's easy to attach too much of our identity to the fact we are musicians.

I'm not saying there is anything wrong with identifying as a total songwriter or performer. The problem becomes when the persona you've built up hinders you from progressing in your career and provide you a sustainable income so you can live the life you want to live. We will often identify so strongly with something, that we will start to adapt social norms that may or may not serve our goals and dreams.

The metal community is a great example of that. Since about the mid-2000's, metal and rock have started to fall out of the mainstream. There used to be a "Best Hard Rock Act" award at the Grammys that was fully televised. Now rock and metal are lucky is they get any feature at all. Even when Metallica joined the stage with Lady Gaga in 2017, and we finally thought that rock and metal would at least get some kind of recognition. James Hetfield, the singer and rhythm guitarist, had no signal from his mic for at least half the performance.

So as you can imagine, the metal and rock community has always been a bit cynical about the mainstream music industry. However, the problem is that the fans and the artists have this sort of toxic, closed-minded elitism that everything that comes out of the mainstream is "over-produced", "fast food music", etc.

But they also feel that their genre of music, which hasn't changed (or evolved) hardly in 20 years, is somehow better and "the masses are just too dumb to get our music" even though is the same watered down versions of bands we've already heard before. This close-minded approach to mainstream acts has actually closed off a lot of artists in the metal community from really great marketing strategies and ways to take advantages of the new digital age.

If I had to pick any genre that I hear the most complaining about having to post on TikTok or start to build their own audience, it's always the metal community. Now I'm not saying all this just to hate on the metal community. I'm trying to show that if we get too wrapped up in our persona or what is considered "acceptable" by the gatekeepers of a genre, we can arbitrarily close ourselves off from things that would otherwise be beneficial to our lives and our music businesses.

Never let social proof and ego determine what strategies you should take in your music business. Results rule, period. You can hate on any genre you want, but if it's popular, there's probably a reason and a lesson to be learned from it.

If you identify too much as a certain type of musician, then you will shut yourself out from opportunities that could help boost your career. It's time to dive into each of these perspectives a little deeper and outline where these go wrong and how you can avoid being too one sided.

All About The Art

"Art is a jealous mistress, and if a man has a genius for painting, poetry, music, architecture, or philosophy, he makes a bad husband, an ill provider, and should be wise in season."
—*Ralph Waldo Emerson*

I'm starting with this imbalance because it's where I found myself in the beginning. I remember spending hours upon hours researching music theory concepts until I was blue in the face. I would dive into things like "Negative Harmony" & "Tonal Symmetry" without understanding how I was going to turn this into something the average listener would want to hear. I would sit there and stress about why my sweep picking wasn't as good as my heroes. Now, some of that no doubt made me a better player because I constantly worked on my craft.

The problem became that I had all these marketable skills, but no skills on how to market those abilities. When I was starting out I figured that was for the labels to worry about because that wasn't my responsibility. This mindset led me and my family supporting me to become the victims of all the common rip offs that you run into when you're trying to become a professional. I remember going to LA try to make contacts even though I lived in Oklahoma. Trying to join "Guitar Brotherhoods" because somehow that would be how I was recognized for my talents (lol). As a consequence, I was the patsy who payed the price for trying to shortcut hard work by paying for it. This leads me to the first problem that artists who are all about the art run into, being the patsy in the room.

Don't Be The Patsy

Warren Buffet said, "if you've been playing poker for half an hour, and you don't know who the patsy in the room is, you're the patsy".

Some people may not see this as a problem. They may say "Dax, what's wrong about wanting to know my craft and having a great relationship with my art?", to which I would say "Nothing!". The problem becomes when you've built your craft up to the point where you can put together a solid tune every now and again, and it's time to go to the next phase in your career where you need to get known and start to build your audience and you don't.

Instead, the "all about the art" types will start to binge on more semantic content that they know already or explore niche concepts they have no intention to incorporate into their existing sound. This type of behavior comes from a few things, the first is fear.

I want to tell you a story because I think it will illustrate my point. I knew a band in my local scene that seriously had the talent and the sound to get known and crush it. They even had a great live show and as a result we would try to have them on our bills whenever we could.

However, there was a hesitance in the band to fully commit to the business and just double down on the perspective that "we're all about the music". There was a big problem, and this is a big problem for newcomers in the music business.

You can't just be "all about the music" and try to pursue a serious career as a musician, because you will inevitably have to operate within the business, and the business is expensive.

Especially when you don't know how to take advantage of your release to make some money, then things become really expensive because you're got nothing to show for your release. You need to have a plan when you release something, you can't just hope for success, you have to make it happen.

They wrote great songs that no mass of people ever really got to hear, and eventually went on indefinite hiatus. That is the exact opposite of what any band would want, and I'm hoping to show you how to avoid this fate for your band.

When you don't have business-sense, it means you're essentially naive to how your industry works and how the players within it really make money. I want to give you an example of what not understanding business sense can get you into.

Every artist has an earnest, yet slightly arrogant feeling that their art is next-level or ground-breaking and is just waiting to be discovered and then the world will catch up to how incredible their music is.

We'll think all we need is that "one big break" from someone in the "higher-ups" who can reach their hand down and swoop us up from the underground and put us into packed venues with raging and roaring fans.

These are mere mirages that serve to maintain a narrative that leads new, naive artists down a road that will cost them thousands of dollars and leave them right where they started. I remember when I heard a manager (who was really selling me on his service) say "wow you guys really have potential to make it", I felt so proud.

I felt like I had finally gotten the recognition I deserved and worked so hard for and that if this person believed the same thing that they would work hard to get us amazing opportunities. For $300 a month for a little under a year, we got one sponsorship and we were the ones who got the sponsorship against the advice of the manager.

That sponsorship was actually framed as "not worth it", but we went for it on our own and got it. It was an entry level sponsorship for an amplifier company named Mesa Boogie. We eventually saw that we weren't getting our moneys worth and fired that manager.

We learned a hard lesson that day, which was don't always trust people who prop you up. They're most likely trying to make you think they're the "one big break" you were looking for and they are far from it.

There was a paradigm shift once streaming started to kick into gear, and that was when tons of people who used to work these A&R type positions, for example, at big labels were getting laid off and there were all kinds of people who were in the business who served a particular function back in the day but now were facing uncertain employment amidst the huge changes in the market.

Well, instead of adapting and finding more ways to provide genuine value to someone, some of these "professionals" decided to trick or convince artists who had not peaked behind the curtain of the business side of the music industry before working with them. They then syphon as much money from the artist as they can, making sure to let you know they did all they can do but it just didn't work out.

The Radio Insider

One very pernicious tactic was accidentally revealed to me one time after a gig in Iowa by the head of a label. He was a bit intoxicated and started rambling to me about how they have a guy "on the inside" in radio who they pay to spike their artists spins so they can get those artists on these secondary market charts.

Of course the label would never tell you that's what they did, they tell you that the song has been doing great and stations seem to really like it according to the chart positions. You know…the same chart positions they just paid for from their inside guy.

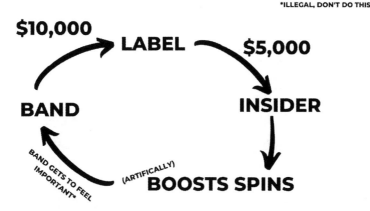

So if a label try to ask $20,000 or $10,000 for a radio campaign, turn and run away as fast as you can. They're most likely going to use $5,000 OR $10,000 of that money to rig your spin stats. Another big red flag is when you're starting out, and people start talking about going in and spending a whole bunch of money recording a single that they're going to send to radio.

This is an old out-dated tactic, you're most likely dealing with a former professional who hasn't changed their old ways and are either knowingly or unknowingly deceiving you.

Hopefully you now have a clearer perspective as to how people can use your naiveness against you when you're trying to get your business going. I've certainly got my own black eyes to account for this, but that doesn't mean you have to go and get yours.

Theres no rule that says paying your dues means paying a bunch of shady people to pretend to help you while servicing your ego. Too many of these situations I've previously mentioned can build up and start to change your association with the business-side of this industry to something negative.

This will prevent you even more from taking action to actually learn how all this business stuff works, but you should view these lessons as a way to keep as much of your money as possible so you can put it to use on things that actually will help you move closer to becoming financially free. However to be financially free, you need capital.

Getting More Options

One of the big side effects of being all about the art is usually a lack a funds or capital. Capital is required to either record/mix/master your music, film a music video, put out new merch, or any other kind of creative project you'd like to do that involves your band. There are very few profit-generating things you can do completely for free.

So let me ask you, which band would you like to be a fan of: a band that releases an album once every 3-4 years, or a band that releases singles or EPs every 3-4 months? I personally would like some new music on a regular basis instead of having to listen to the same music for almost half a decade before I get something new from artists I enjoy.

When you don't have a descent business that provides you even a basic amount of money, it can lead to these very long release times. These long release times can cause fans to become tired of hearing the same old songs from you, and start listening to the bands that have new material out.

You want to keep people in your ecosystem for as long a period as possible, and when you're releasing music on a regular basis it's easier to keep people involved in what you are doing. If you look at the rap and hip-hop genre, they're excellent at keeping fans engaged with the culture of their brand because they're always putting out music or have lots of opportunities to support for their fans.

Speaking of quality, there is definitely one place you shouldn't skimp out on: and that's your audio production. I remember when my band, Kirra, went to record our full-length record with Gabe and I had recently learned some of the ropes of audio production. It was real rudimentary information. We decided to save a bunch of money by having me record the record 75% at my place, and 25% at a studio for the drums (because I wasn't about to add that to my already huge workload of producing/mixing the record).

Well, I was initially in way over my head and it led to a less than high-quality production of the record. Sadly, I learned techniques that would have solved 90% of my mixing issues about 5 months after the record was finished. Isn't that always how it works?

The point is, when you're not focusing on your business you have less capital, which at its heart means one thing: you have less options. There are certainly ways to not break the bank when recording a song or an EP, but you want to make sure that the quality is good enough for one group of people, your fans.

I don't care if your label doesn't dig the mix, I don't care if your mom or dad doesn't like the mix, as long as the fans are receiving something that they would enjoy, you are in the right place.

I'd recommend having some people who you know are fans but trust their opinion and are trust-worthy with early access to music. You need some outside ears to give you some straight forward advice.

One big tip is to divide who you get your constructive criticism from into 3 categories: people who are right where you are in their career, people who are where you want to be, and people who want to be where you are.

LAW OF 33%

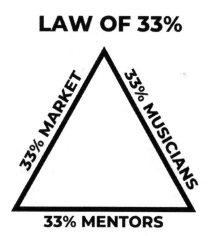

33% MENTORS

Each group will have their own biases, but combined can give you a clearer perspective on any changes that you may need to implement.

For one of my bands releases we got advice from our label, our trusted fans, and some friends in the local scene. The label thought that we needed to cut a verse out of our song and were very passionate with that position because they were trying to follow an "industry standard" of getting to the first chorus by 30 seconds.

The trusted fans thought the verse sounded fine, and the peers thought the bridge droned on a bit. So what did we do? We decided to cut a section of the bridge for radio and make the label do two versions with no edits. By having everyones perspective we were able to make the most informed decision possible.

Focusing On Your Image

One of the other downsides to being all about the art is that it's more pain-staking to form your band's brand. A lot of musicians just want to wear whatever they want, have the photographer do all the work, and hope for the best when the final proofs are sent.

There was one band that was showing me their pics and they were mad because one of the members wore shorts and basically looked like he'd just left an 8th grade social studies class. This was for a metal shoot, so the rest of the band had on dark jeans, dark shirts, and looked generally serious. Then there was the one dude smiling in his basketball shorts and threw the whole vibe of the shoot.

Apparently nobody agreed upon what image they were all going for and some intuited the right look and another just took it as a cue to do whatever. Because of this low-quality and in-cohesive look, their brand failed to grab any awareness or traction and they eventually had to start over by remaking the band and rearranging members.

To be clear, they didn't just fire a guy over shorts, there had been a history of behavior that had prompted the firing. However, they did have to restart which killed their momentum, and led to slower growth.

What is a brand and why do people need to be aware of it? A brand is simply a unified look that serves as a unique marker that establishes your band as its own cohesive entity. Whenever you're trying to build a cohesive brand, you want to make sure that everything looks cohesive, whatever the theme may be.

Use your creativity to explore different themes, but once you all come to a collective conclusion on a theme, stick with it. Make sure if you're a country artist, that you give off an authentic-to-you country look.

If you're a pop artist, stick out by using your unique portrait to enhance your release.

Rock and metal artists have more of a general aesthetic (lots of black), with lots of subtle variations in-between. You can hopefully see that the most effective way to establish your brand is to have cohesion in your image.

Take a look at some of your favorite artists and see what themes they've experimented with throughout their career. You'll probably find some cool ideas to expand upon, as well as see what might have been "trendy" at the time and therefore might be dated.

There is a little diagram I want to show you so you can start to build your brand with ease using 4 simple components I call the building blocks of branding!

It starts with colors, what are the different colors you're going to use. These colors should remain consistent through your merchandise, website, social media avatars & banners, etc. Colors will be very important in the beginning phases of your career and will give people an association to your particular brand.

Colors don't have to be a permanent commitment. A lot of times colors will shift and change based on the release you've got coming up next. My band would, for instance, change the colors and themes but we would keep the same logo and signature symbol that is associated with our brand.

BUILDING BLOCKS OF BRANDING

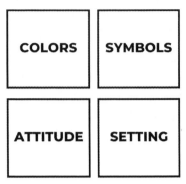

Which brings me to my next component, symbols. Your logo and symbol are very similar. Think of your logo as your band name in a recognizable font or design. Your symbol however is like a shorthand version of your logo that could be on things like social media avatars, stickers, etc.

My band's name is KIRRA (and yes the capitalization is on purpose because it looks more like our logo), and when we were getting started, we were thinking of some different ways to make that a unique and recognizable brand. We eventually decided on flipping the second R in the name to a reverse Я. This turned our logo into KIRЯA in a particular font that made the R's look really cool next to each other like that.

If this was what we came up with for our logo, then what would our symbol be? Well we decided on "RЯ". This double facing R became our signature, and we put this branding on all of our merchandise, we made it all of our social media avatars, and we even put it on the front of our kick drum.

Once you've got a great set of symbols and colors, you've got a great foundation to start promoting your brand. However, the next two are designed to fine-tune your brand to upgrade it to the level of what pros have. The next block is setting or the theme. You can have a consistent brand with a set logo/symbol evolving colors and evolving settings.

Themes are supposed to make your idea pop! Whatever your single title, your album, or even your tour flyer is, you want the images and designs that are on everything to be right on theme with the theme of your music. This is why artwork is so crucial to an effective and infectious brand, because it serves as a setting for your branding. Weezer would often have album covers that look identical accept for the colors and clothes they wear. This made a Weezer album very easy to discern on a shelf full of other records.

If you were wondering, clothes are apart of your branding and I consider it part of the setting. Sometimes with a new release, a new wardrobe or hairdo can do wonders to help accentuate the theme of a particular release. Importantly, this will separate the themes of releases and make them easier to remember which specific song or album they were listening to. You'll hear people say "oh its the red and black album where they're all wearing x", or "oh yeah, that's the pink and white album cover".

Each setting, accompanied by the title and lyrics, will give each release a certain vibe and attitude. This brings me to the last part of building your brand as an artist, which is your attitude. Your attitude really has a lot to do with presentation. We've talked about everything around you including your clothes, but this last one is about you. How do you carry yourself? Are you smiling or are you frowning (because metal)? Are you using sex appeal (no matter how subtle)?

I know, some of these things are a little silly to think about, but funny enough they actually can really be the final selling point to a release. If you have a laid back acoustic release coming out, it's probably not a great idea to smash the guitar on the ground while throwing up the rock horns for your promo photos. Make sense?

You want everyone in your band to be on the same page as to what they feel the band's image should look like. If people don't want to start committing to these more business-type actives like putting together a brand as well as putting together offers for your fans, building a sales process and different suites of products for your fans to enjoy and things of the like, you may have someone who isn't entirely committed to becoming a professional musician.

It's a lot like when you get involved in a relationship, everyone avoids the uncomfortable reality of accepting getting into a relationship. Which is "we are either going to stay together forever, or break up". It's very similar with a band.

You're either going to commit to practice and form a sound, get that sound out to people, and start to set up your fundamental business systems, or you're going to disband or go into hiatus. You can have multiple projects that you have commitments to, but you want to make sure you can actually fulfill all of your obligations.

The music business is inside of the entertainment industry, and the entertainment industry is a very superficial one. You can unknowingly lose gigs to people who don't have near the talent you do because they had a bit more style in their wardrobe than you. I know there are artists out there who find it vain in someway if you pay too much attention to your looks, and while there are definitely cases of artists being very vain and self-centered. There are plenty (if not more) cases of artists using a fair bit of light fashion to help really give yourself that "professional" look.

If you have someone you know who has a passion for fashion (unintentional rhyme), then you should inquire for their advice to improve your wardrobe. When it comes to what I wear when I'm working or on the road in between shows, I dress for comfort and function. When I'm on stage, have to perform in a video shoot or take some promotional photos, I'm dressing for the brand that I have created with the guys in my band.

All About The Money

*"For the love of money people can't even walk the street,
because they never know who in the world they're gonna
beat for that lean, mean, mean green almighty dollar"*
—*The O'Jays*

When artists finally recognize that there's merit to learning how the business works so they can become more entrepreneurial, they run into the problem of escaping a 9-5, to turn music into their 9-5. This defeats the purpose of being an entrepreneur. We are trying to create not only financial freedom, but we're trying to get our time back as well. So when you start to turn your music into a business, beware of turning your music into a job. It's something that people don't realize they're doing because they're used to working in 9-5 jobs so they don't know how to treat their music any other way.

The other side of this coin is the artist who gets some financial success and some of their time back, but now they're just treating something that had a lot of personal value to something that they use to get more money and access more vices. The music is no longer art to them, it becomes a vehicle to fulfill the ego. This is something any musician needs to look out for because of how incentives act like gravity. We'll touch on that more later. For now, I want to dive into what happens when artists become all about the money and lose sight on what really matters.

Losing Sight On What Matters

We've all heard of those bands or artists who make their music solely for the purpose of material gains, and really don't care how formulaic their music becomes as long as people stream it and they get payed the big bucks. These artists tend to only be able to write in a style that inflates their own ego and exaggerates their personas to almost the point of losing a true sense of identity.

This perspective of only being about the money can also lead to an unhealthy relationship with your fans, treating them just as profit centers and not as human beings that are possibly being transformed by your music. I'm going to break down the main pitfalls of viewing music solely through the lens of profit without concern of the quality of the art being produced.

One time I remember doing some research into other artists who were in my genre (2000s style radio hard rock), and I wanted to see who the A-list players were and who the B-listers were all the way down to the people that just barley got a modicum of success and faded into obscurity.

I noticed a pretty common trend among the artists who were the mainstream acts and the people who couldn't seem to get any traction, and it was something pretty simple. The bands that were the most successful had their own unique sound that was pretty distinguishable, and the bands who faded into obscurity almost seemed like watered-down, cosplayed versions of those same mainstream, legacy acts.

There was no attempt at innovation with these obscure artists and a lot of their music was one-dimensional. These bands would either fade away or completely change their sound to something that's unrecognizable from their previous efforts.

This is one of the pitfalls of making music just to ride a trend. You make something to catch a wave, then you get pigeon-holed into a category that you aren't innovating in, and often you get bands that just get burned-out after not seeing any progress or evolution.

There are ways to divide these bands up whenever a trend comes out and takes over the mainstream consciousness. I divide them into three categories: 1) The OGs (Trend Setters), these are the artists that pioneer a sound. These artists may not have been the most popular bands of the trends era, sometimes they are, but sometimes they just provide the bedrock for the sound that is evolving.

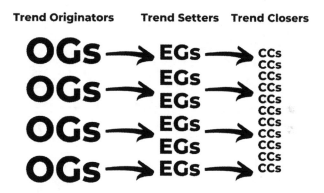

For example, there was a band that came out the Seattle area in 1984 named, Green River, who were the earliest known example of the "grunge" sound as it later became known. The band even had members that later went on to perform inside the bands that are synonymous with the Seattle grunge era. This is an example of an OG, but what about the bands that pushed the sound to wide-spread adoption and acceptance.

This next category of artists are the EGs (Trend Setters). EGs stand for Explosion G's, these are artists who became the faces of a trend by staying on top of a mainstream wave for at least 5 years. These artists usually had broad worldwide commercial success and are generally associated with the trend itself whenever mentioned.

If I continue to use my Seattle grunge example, the EGs would be bands like Pearl Jam, Nirvana, Alice in Chains, and Soundgarden. There were even a couple of bands like Stone Temple Pilots and Smashing Pumpkins that managed to break out and be trend setters of this era. They may not have founded the sound, but they popularized it. The final category is what we need to avoid unless you want to cosplay other more successful artists.

One thing you can do is make sure you're not *just* making music to catch a trend, now if you're genuinely able to contribute to a trend in an innovative way that might be worth your while. However, throwing together a compilation of worn-out tactics while desperately trying to get people to notice your band since people aren't noticing you for the art you've been previously creating, never comes across well.

You may get some fans of people who just like one particular sound and instead of expanding their musical palate, decide to go the opposite direction and dive deeper into the back catalogues of bands who attempted to create that sound they love so much, no matter how blatantly contrived and commercial. Attempting to cosplay your favorite artists in hopes of literally stealing their fan base will inevitably lead to stale art.

There are artists in the rock genre at the moment who are quite literally cosplaying a band known as, Led Zeppelin. I won't throw them under the bus by-name, but I'm sure you can get the reference if you are in the rock-world.

I don't want to insinuate that the previously mentioned band is just doing it for the money, but what I'm hinting at is that to by-default resort to cosplaying your heroes is a clear show of a lack of confidence and can borderline copying. This will give fans or listeners the impression that you are unoriginal and probably therefore all about the money, even if this is intended by the band or not.

Breaking The Hail Mary Mindset

This cosplay, copycat syndrome is driven by the next mindset that is absolutely toxic as an upcoming artist, and this is the "Hail Mary" mindset. I remember one time I was trying to figure out the most effective steps I could take in my band to get it off the ground and get masses of people to notice.

I figured all I need was that one viral video, that one label to believe in us, that one radio campaign to be successful, that one ad that converted like crazy, and all these other "one things" that if they happened, we would have officially "made it" and have tons of fans that would support us.

These desires were all predicated on this toxic Hail Mary mindset, the idea that there was one vehicle that would take the band to new heights instead of good old fashioned independent marketing and good songwriting. The reality is that there isn't ONE thing that's going to give you millions of fans or finally "make it". It's going to be a long process of you continually engaging your existing fans while putting together awesome songs to get you some new ones.

This process can be supercharged with certain business strategies we'll discuss later, but having the mindset that once you get a great manager, work with a label, or find a booking agent that your career troubles will all be solved and you can relax and just go back to only worrying about music is wrong.

You will always have to be involved on some level in the business side of your music career, and understanding that it's the people that realistically talk about incremental progress and consistent engagement that are the ones you want to listen to in regards to running your music business.

There is nothing wrong with scaling once you've found a system that works, but dropping big sums of cash in the early stages looking for that one long-shot that's going to make your bands career is a big fat waste of time.

I remember a band that invested thousands of dollars into a super high definition music video, they got a van, booked a bunch of traveling dates, and their music was like nails on a chalkboard. I understand musical taste has a great layer of subjectivity to it, but this was objectively bad and clearly trying to hop on a pop trend. They started paying a manager $300 per month to give them more opportunities.

You know what they didn't do? Build a local following, put together cool deals and offers for their fans, or put out music often. They were trying to condense their entire career into a few moves and a year or so. Need less to say, this band disbanded very quickly.

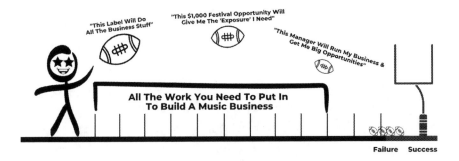

The Hail Mary mindset is really predicated on a bunch of selfish and narcissistic ideas that all serve to prop up our sense of self-importance by being able to say to the other bands in our scene that "we're signed" or "we have a manager".

I'm going to tell you the dirty little secret now, there is no *one*, singular way to have success in this business. That's true for any business for that matter. There are managers who will tell you about all the different big contacts they either knew back in the day, managed for short period of time, or "are good friends with" (meaning they met them once at a show or convention).

There are tons of labels that will promise they'll get you onto the radio and that you'll break into the charts. There are plenty of radio campaign coordinators who will charge you thousands of dollars to pester their mediocre contacts for you while promising your all these spins and listeners.

There are plenty of festival operators promising "huge exposure" and a great audience when they haven't drawn more than 100 people since 1997. All of these Hail Mary opportunities have a predictable cycle: the hype, the cliffhanger, the fall. The hype is the phase where they start building up your ego and start telling you things that appeal to your ego or desire for growth.

This is where the slick-talkers come out and tell you all about how this particular opportunity is going to be the single cause to either your whole success, or at least a really big boost in your current stage of your career. The cliffhanger is the build up to the day of the results that were promised. Whether that's the build up to a show, the day a manager was going to talk to someone big, the day the label executive had a meeting with some big suits, or even the first day your get a radio spin report back and see what your music has done.

Finally, there is the fall. This is the phase where you realize that these people weren't able to give you the overnight success you were implicitly or explicitly requesting from them, and that it was either a waste of time, it was a waste of money, or it was both. This leads you exactly where you were before the hype phase but just a bit more broke now while some slick talker who knew how to exploit your Hail Mary mindset walked away with your money.

I remember once when I was coming up, and was promised an opportunity to play a festival down in Florida, and this was a pretty big festival so we were really excited about the opportunity to be on the same bill as some leaders in our genre. If you're wondering where the catch is, we found out that this opportunity would cost us $1,000.

By this point, we've had days where we could make $1,000 in one days worth of merch sales, and we figured that if we are at a festival that has thousands of people then we probably have a great chance of making our money back and getting tons of fans as a consequence.

Makes sense, right? Well, there were some things that were conveniently omitted from discussion when we were deciding whether or not to take this opportunity. The first being that the promoter we were getting this opportunity through was not directly associated to the festival, but had payed money to rent out space NEXT to the festival to put up their own stage so they could LOOK like they were apart of the festival.

They weren't associated with the festival though, and as a consequence, our merchandise was actually to the left of this stage we had payed to be at and not with all the other artists who had hour long lines to their merch table. So our merch was about 200 yards away from the main merch traffic.

So not only did we not have the kind of audience the bands INSIDE the festival had, but we got a tiny amount of merch traffic which made it to where we lost money on the opportunity. This started out as a huge opportunity to debut our new single at a festival and make some decent progress, and it ended up being a 40 hour drive to get basically none of the things we were promised.

If you get taken advantage of enough times, it will turn you very cynical about this business and inevitably ruin your relationship with it. You've got to stop focusing on Hail Mary's and start focusing on incremental, exponential growth over time.

This time should not be wasted wishing and hoping things are going to happen, but actually using this time in your early career development to start building the foundations you will need once things start to pick up. If you know how to manage a little, you can manage a lot. However, if you can't even manage a little, you won't all of a sudden become great at managing money just because you have more of it now.

You have to commit to engaging your fans while giving them great art, content, and valuable offers they can take to support you. This money will be then able to be invested into your music business aka back into the fans experience.

However, if you're focused on becoming an overnight success without having to do any of the ground work, you're going to overlook this in your business and you will use the success as a way to serve yourself without serving the fans. This is one terrible side-effect of this mindset and the effects of it playing out on an artist over and over again, and its how the fans get treated inevitably throughout this process.

Forgetting Why Your Business Exists

Whenever you're solely focused on yourself and growth, you can very easily forget about the fans you have and treat them less than ideal. Your mindset really impacts how you treat people.

If all you care about is getting money from people, whenever you're interacting with them at the merch booth let's say for example, you won't be able to fully be present with that fan and get to know them. You'll just be figuring out how you can get them to buy and if they don't buy you'll kind of just wish they would walk away so you can try again with the next person.

Now don't get me wrong, there are ways to build that rapport with your fans and still sell them. However, when you start from the base of being all about the money, you will instinctually avoid building genuine rapport.

Just like a McDonalds cashier doesn't really build rapport with the person ordering the food because they're just there for a paycheck and don't really care. Avoid your fan/artist dynamic from turning into this, you need to care.

These people are potentially going to be the people that support you for the rest of your life, don't sacrifice that relationship for monetary gains in the short term.

I've seen bands that have this all-about-the-money attitude and treat their fans like crap. I remember being on tour with this band and every night the lead singer would hit on the female audience members without shame, it was appalling to see. No artist would treat their fans like that if they actually respected them or if they truly understood the value they have. I watched fans that had loved this band, immediately swear off the band for good because of the treatment she had received by the singer.

You never know the butterfly effect that could be set into motion by one really mistreated fan. Don't use fans to service your ego. I know it can be tempting when you showered with compliments after a really good gig, but remain humble and don't think of fans as means to ends, but as people who receive value from your music.

Seeing fans as means to ends like your mansion or Lamborghini is not only unethical in my opinion, but is also unhealthy for your own mental well-being. This type of thinking can lead to isolation from your peers because you don't actually form those genuine bonds with people because you'll again just see them as more means to more ends.

There was one singer I was on the same tour with who only viewed people as sources of money and when people would come up to his merch table, he would never greet them or frankly say anything to them. He was probably one of the most anti-social lead singers I had ever seen.

He would only talk to the females and the men he would only talk to if they wanted to buy something. We didn't work with him very long but I'll never forget the feeling of never wanting to treat my fans like that, because he was not a happy person and that wasn't who I was trying to become. Don't emulate the traits from people you would not want to become. I've seen people just start doing things a certain way because someone they admired did it that way, but what they didn't know, was how it goes down behind the scenes. Then the strategies that seemed like tried and true, turn into out dated ways of the past very quick.

Protecting Your Relationship With Music

You never get into this business thinking that it could hurt your love for music, but you'd be surprised how many artists hurt the relationship they have with their art and view it was more of a job than anything else. Its really sad to see this because no musician wants this, it's a sign of someones spirit and enthusiasm that has been broken down.

When your only source of income comes from an out-dated way of running your music business, it's very easy to view being in a band as just a job.

Road dogs grinding and touring just to keep their head afloat. I've been on tours where I see how people can get if they've had some success but to maintain the lifestyle they've built, they have to tour 250+ shows per year.

Since they aren't what they used to be, they don't get paid as much which meant that they had to tour more to maintain their lifestyle. It's a vicious cycle and if caught in this trap, can damage your relationship to something that is supposed to be fulfilling.

So yes, you need to make money in order to keep everything running smoothly. However, if you become to unbalanced and focused solely on profit, you will have effectively left one rat-race for another. You will have a very difficult time connecting with people because when someone is all about the money, people can sense it.

Incentives are like gravity or a tornado, they pull everything near closer to them. If you have an incentive in your life that makes music the prime way you're keeping your lights on, then you're going to make music like a job. That's how people view jobs, places they have to go to do stuff so they can keep the lights on and fed well.

INCENTIVES

Fans are not stupid, they will see right through you if you are being unauthentic and trying to pull one over on them. Make sure you set up your business systems in ways that don't put you in a position that in order to make more income, it will require you to exchange your time 1:1 for that income.

Set up your systems that will require your time *initially*, but once the system is in place will require little to no maintenance and give you your time back. Failing to do this can lead to the rat-race mentality that a lot of professional musicians fall prey to once they get some success like I mentioned earlier.

It's like at your job. Your boss wants you to live slightly above your means, that way you're incentivized to come in and work to get the money to maintain this lifestyle you've been enabled to create by your boss. Well in music, the same thing can happen.

Don't be so focused on material things that you build a lifestyle that is unsustainable. Sit down and actually outline what a perfect day would look like for you, to the very last detail. What would you think about when you wake up? What would your morning routine look like? Who would you be with when all this is happening? This isn't new-age woo.

This is clearly seeing in your mind the desired result, and gearing your goals and actions to reach that specific desired result. If you don't know exactly where you want to go, you're walking blind.

I remember once, John Mayer told an audience of Berklee College of Music students in Boston, MA a story about a friend he had that sold over 2,000,000 records, and they were completely miserable. Can you imagine that? You've worked so hard for years to build up some success for yourself and you can't even enjoy it!

You might be thinking to yourself "well not me! I would be happy sell 2,000,000 records", and I bet you probably would. However, if you haven't told yourself "if I sell 2,000,000 records then I've definitely 'made it'", then I would argue you might not be as happy and fulfilled as you think.

Expectation and precision of your goals is absolutely essential to success in any field of work. A lot of our perception is relative. The person who only sells 100 records a year thinks the person who sells 1,000,000 records a year is someone who hung the moon. However, the person who sells 1,000,000 records looks at the artist who is selling 10,000,000 records and thinks *they* hung the moon.

So what happens as you cross past your initial success milestones, you're going to feel a great sense of pride and accomplishment. I can guarantee this will be followed very soon by this feeling of wanting to take things to the next level, setting your eyes up higher at a bigger goal that you actually have the knowledge and skills to attain now. This is the cyclical process of success that is inevitable whenever you start to see progress in your music business.

I remember when I stepped onto the stage of a House of Blues in Chicago and looked out to see a sea of about 1,500 people stacked three floors high while we were opening up for a national touring act. Having remembered the days where we spent hours in a cramped van and playing empty gigs for $16, looking out and seeing the sea of faces before me and the joy on their faces as we went through our set was one of my first moments of realizing I had crossed a milestone in my career.

As you can imagine, I was on quite the adrenaline rush of having just played one of the biggest shows in my entire career up to that point. However, very soon after playing around 6 different House of Blues across the US, I started to set my sights on bigger venues. I wanted to experience the same thing but in a huge theatre. As quickly as that moment of pride came, it was replaced just as quickly with a sense of ambition to get to the next step, halving seen that I could bring myself to this milestone to begin with.

Identifying your different milestones will give smaller wins on the way to your bigger wins. This will keep the fire in you strong, and make it less likely for you to get industry burn-out. There is nothing worse than working for years and feeling like you're stuck in the mud and making no progress, that is what kills musicians momentum more than anything else.

This is why there are musicians that sell 2,000,000 albums who are miserable. How could that possibly be? It's because they never defined what exactly "making it" meant and therefore, nothing was ever enough for them. They passed through milestone after milestone without ever really taking the time to acknowledge them, and therefore appreciate those little wins. This is the power of precisely defining where you want to go.

Finding Balance

"If you correct your mind, your life will fall into place."
—Lao Tzu

It's time to get into becoming balanced in your art and in your business. We need to break down what strategies you'll need to have a proper perspective of both your art from a business perspective and your business from the perspective of a musician. Understanding each of these perspectives is like the yin yang.

You don't want to be one-sided in your perceptions about how to run your music business effectively. In my experience, I see two types of musicians: 1) you have the "all about the money" group. They only write music, play shows, and sell merch for the sole purpose of making a buck.

People who have this mindset are rarely concerned with pushing boundaries and want to stick in a comfort zone and often result to copying because they think that's either all that will sell or it's all they have committed to learning.

If you're lazy in your art and active in your business, you are being all about the money. 2) you have the "all about the art" group of musicians, and if I was going to bet, I would assume that is most likely the larger portion of musicians abroad. These musicians don't care to learn a single thing about the business-world or finance because "that's what stiffs do", "that's all corrupt", or "that isn't cool".

There's plenty more excuses people put in their own way but those are by far the most common. Often, these type of musicians are consumed with the art and obsess over all the semantic details of their craft instead of learning how to get their music seen by more people. They'll learn the craziest possible progressive-jazz chords possible or how they can get their tone closer to their heroes and buy thousands of dollars worth of equipment chasing that sound.

Don't misunderstand, both of these sides have partial truths to them. However, I find that finding what is good in both sides and figuring out ways to balance them and integrate the opposites of what you're used into your personality are essential keys to developing a more balanced perspective of both music and business. Below, I put a chart together demonstrating more clearly the idea I'm trying to show you when I said you need to view this like a yin yang.

Each side will have its strengths and its weaknesses, but the goal is to balance each approach whenever pursuing a career in music. Without balance, it's inevitable that one will start to dominate and then you will start to see the side effects of this imbalance. Take a look at each side and figure out how you can better integrate these forces in your music business.

Yin/Art	Yang/Business
Self Expression	Growth
Entropy	Sustainability
Cyclical	Perpetual
No Rules	Laws & Rules
Goodwill	Profit
Spontaneous	Systematic
Competition	Collaboration

-Self Expression-

Self-expression is one of the main forces that drives a lot of musicians to create. We audibly hear an idea in our head, we see or visualize something that inspires us, we experience something that changes us, and we imagine what is possible. The art that we create is a direct representation of what we are trying to express.

This is a force with tremendous power because it is where we attach a lot of our identity as artists. When we want to express love into our art, we will access the parts of ourselves that have associations to love, or when we want to express anger we will access that parts of ourselves that have associations to anger.

Depending on what genre you want to express, you might represent yourself differently. That's why you could probably tell the average country fan from the average heavy metal fan. The guy with long black hair and all black clothing probably doesn't like Luke Bryan. He might! People are very diverse in their tastes, but if we are the artists representing the music for example, we probably fit more into these identifiable roles.

The force of self expression can be corrupted, however, when things become only about self-expression the ego can begin to grow past its usefulness. You will often see this with artists who are obsessed with being unique, niche, or avant-garde then start to believe that anything associated with cultural forces are harmful to self-expression.

In some senses, this impulse is right, because culture is often a very rigid force upon people. It doesn't like "out-of-the-box" type behavior or ideas. We often forget though that sometimes, that isn't really a bad thing. We don't need people who are being avant-garde with architecture, that's how you get buildings and bridges to collapse.

We need to be able to balance being prolific enough to stand out but not so out there that we alienate the majority of people who interact with us. I know there are probably some artists reading this that are getting mad at what I'm saying, and that's okay. The way you can do this in a well-balanced manner so that you don't sacrifice your artistic uniqueness is to rid yourself of overtly one-sided, extreme ideologies.

There are extremes that people can adopt in their life as a desperate means of self-expression, and the cheapest way is to be "anti-establishment" or "anti-conformity" for their own sakes. This represents the artists who aren't "anti" any particular establishment, just anti-establishment in general. What happens when people telling you not conform, have their own brand of conformity?

These people often just think their own version of conformity is better than cultures current version of conformity. The common thread among the purists in this area of art, is due in-part in the name of self-expression.

I remember a time in my life where I was very rigid in my musical tastes, and I was dumping on all the modern pop acts of the time (or any act that used overly modern production or heavily processed sounds). I thought "if it doesn't come from guitar, bass, drums, and vocals then it's somehow 'cheap' or 'cheating'" in some way. I told you I was dumb lol.

Well I was so anti-mainstream that I alienated my tastes from music that was good but also started to notice how much I was being a gatekeeper. I was started to have my own form of conformity that I was imposing on other people, which made me no different than any gatekeeping jerk. The metal community has this sort of elitist strain in it and is completely toxic. Luckily there was a band called Nothing More that actually "converted" me from my rigid tastes by tastefully using electronic elements to hard rock and killer songwriting to accompany it.

The point is not to alienate yourself from people who would be your fan because there is an extreme ideology that is influencing our persona.

-Growth-

What is an effective check on monolithic self-expression? Growth. Growth is very measurable, and it is something that can check if your "new idea that's super unique and cool" is actually as cool as you think it is.

For instance, you may think you've created the next big thing in your genre, but until you go out and test it, you have no idea whether it actually is the next big thing. You need to track your results and you need to run experiments. In life, the one who experiments the most wins because you get data that most people ignore.

Growth has even been identified as one of the key needs of the six basic needs that every human needs. You have four needs of the personality (certainty, variety, love/connection, and significance) and two needs of the spirit (growth and contribution).

The Six Fundamental Human Needs

The Needs of the Personality			
Certainty	Variety	Significance	Love / Connection
Growth		Contribution	
The Needs of the Spirit			

Growth is how you continually make progress. Nothing will kill a music career faster than stagnation. Bands that don't release albums but every half decade or so, never releasing singles, never promoting, etc. This is where entropy starts to kick in, and your music business begins to deteriorate. If you don't water your garden everything dies. The same is true of your music business.

You need to be consciously focused on growth and making sure you're making progress on your goals inside your business and your personal life. I remember there was guitarist I knew who was one of the best musicians in his area. He was always known as the "best" guitar player in all the local circles. The issue was he lived in a small town, and once he moved to the big city and met musicians in our local area he started to see that he wasn't really as amazing as he had built up in his ego.

Now, when you come across someone who is better than you at something, what is your instinctual reaction? Probably to get a little defensive, right? Now some people get past that initial envy and use it as fire to propel them forward and force them to start working on their skills so they can become closer to what they want their ability or skill to be. Other people get bitter and feel threatened by the success of others and will constantly belittle any accomplishments that make them feel inferior. Which one do you think this guy did?

Unfortunately, he got bitter instead of better. I knew this guy personally, and so I would hear him practice from time to time. Sadly, every time I heard his practice he was always playing the same thing he had always played. He was playing the same songs, the same riff ideas, the same licks, everything was exactly the same.

He would always complain about how he couldn't do things on the guitar or that he wasn't even the best guitar player in his own band and so on. As a result, he never got better and needless to say, his music career went absolutely nowhere. Drummer Chris Coleman once said "you can get bitter or get better", and that always stuck with me to use peoples success as a model and fire that something can be accomplished.

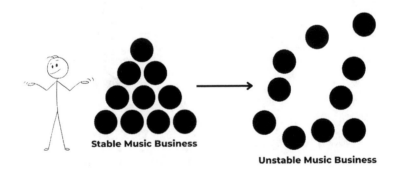

Stable Music Business

Unstable Music Business

-Entropy-

I want to talk about something I mentioned a bit before which is entropy. Entropy is a natural law that things that are unmaintained will divulge into decay and chaos. If you leave a house vacant for a month the house will be covered in dust, there will be spider webs all over the house, and most likely the lawn will start to take back the house. If you put a song out there, but you give it no promotion or any of the things it needs to be maintained, it will fade into obscurity.

This is also true for every aspect of your business. If you don't maintain your marketing, you won't get any new fans. If you don't maintain your songwriting, you won't have any songs. If you don't maintain your sales process, you will have no sales. All these things need your weekly or sometimes daily attention.

-Sustainability-

You need things that are sustainable. Which brings me to the opposite side of entropy, sustainability. Remember this, systems make you sustainable. We are going to go more in-depth to this concept and show you exactly how to make your systems but you need to know that it's not as complicated as it may sound.

How can you book consistent gigs? If you have a system running that gets you shows on autopilot because the system is working how its supposed to, that's great. Once you get to a certain point in your career, you will have a booking agent who has their own system, but until then you need to build your own unless you hate frequent gigs.

Having systems like this inside of your music business will give you access to more sustainability because you're constantly moving, constantly writing, constantly promoting, etc. This will also help you achieve more growth and avoid entropy. Now sometimes things can go up and down in waves in this business, which brings me to the cyclical side of music.

-Cyclical

Trends and preferences among audiences will change, things will go in and out of flavor. Don't be afraid to adapt to changes in what's considered enjoyable by audiences. I'm not saying you need to just copy the top 40 on Spotify at the expense of what you might want to write.

What I am suggesting is that you can analyze that top 40 on Spotify (or Billboard), and see what trends tend to be consistent throughout those top 40 and see what you might be able to integrate naturally into your sound. It could be as simple as particular melodic patterns you're hearing across songs. It could also be as simple as beats or grooves that seem to be popular at that moment.

One of my favorite acts that was able to change with the times successfully, were the Bee Gees. Three brothers managed to kick off a career in the 60's in keeping with "Beatle-mania" that was happening worldwide, and they literally had a breakout song because their first single was sent to a radio station without a band name, hoping the DJ would think it was new Beatles song. Then they marched on into the 70's and basically popularized the disco movement into pop culture so much that radio stations had to start having "Bee Gee Free" days on their station. Songs like "Stayin' Alive" are still played today in movies and referenced in pop culture. That song alone is over 50 years old, isn't that crazy?

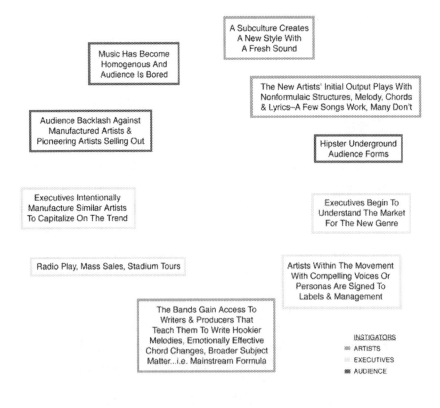

Well as disco fell out of flavor with the masses, the Bee Gees were forced to present something a little bit different. They managed to switch to a more traditional pop sound towards the 80's and even got their second number 1 single in the process for the song "One". They even started to dabble into R&B style's in the 90's. Through each step in this process, the Bee Gees remained relevant powerhouses in the business.

Eventually members started to pass away for various reasons, and the oldest brother Barry now remains as the sole member in Bee Gees and is still putting out music. If you can persevere and adapt through the cycles of the business, you will inevitably have a longer lasting career. Now this is once you've gotten your break into a mass of people (whether or not it's 'mainstream' or not).

-Perpetual-

It's very possible to have a creative take on a popular beat or groove, so no excuses. There are some things that just happen to work, and what's wrong with exercising your creativity to have fresh takes on things that are considered mainstream. This brings me to the perpetual nature of business.

There are some things that will always work like the beat that is considered "the money beat" by session drummers that have made millions playing it. They play this simple drum beat better than anyone else out there, and that's why they get paid the big bucks. It's about mastering the fundamentals more than playing the most advanced things like an amateur.

In business, there are things that are perpetual and will always work. Skills like learning how to market yourself, how to sell, how to hire superstars and a-players, and tons of other skills. This is how you get your competitive edge in this business. Most musicians have no idea about the fundamentals of business and some are even held back by ideological beliefs that have made "business" or "entrepreneurship" a dirty word.

Committing to learning the fundamentals of entrepreneurship is essential to your journey as a professional artist. Don't let strange and new sounding terminology or people (usually with no success of their own) who say "musicians don't do that" hold you back from realizing your full potential and creating a music business most never get.

-No Rules-

When it comes down to it, there is a strong art-component to entrepreneurship, and with art there are no rules. This is where musicians can start to push boundaries and break convention. I've seen some artists figure out how to blend jazz and latin music with metal, I've heard songs that have more than one guitar solo, I've heard songs that have no chorus. Truly, there are no rules when it comes down to your art.

This remains true not just in your art as in your music, but the art that is inside of your business. The only rules you should care about are your countries laws that if you ignore, you will go to jail or rules that will break your morals and values. Outside of those two rules, I wouldn't care to cater too much to convention.

Peter Drucker once said "the only two things business can improve on is innovation and marketing". Innovation could be anything in relation to your songwriting, or it could be anything related to your music business itself.

-Laws & Rules-

Now you need to be a little careful because there are somethings that could get you in a lot of trouble, and that would be if you actually broke the law. If you rip off an artist and benefit from it monetarily, then you could be at risk for a lawsuit and to have all your royalties and earnings taken and penalized further on top of all of that.

However, as long as you're not directly copying melodies, lyrics, and beats exactly as they're performed (even if moved to another key), you should be fine and not have to worry about anything. If you wrote something conversely, and someone rips you off, proving that you are the original creator of a piece of music can be as easy as pulling up the file on your phone where you had the idea and the date attached to it. Some people have gone as far as putting a CD in the mail and mailing themselves a copy just to have it on record go through and be on the grid.

I don't know if you need to take things that far, but it's fairly easy to avoid being ripped off and denied royalties of something you created. There have been some frivolous lawsuits recently in the music business over songs that sound completely different but because they have similar elements like a beat or chord progression, have opened them up to lawsuits. Ed Sheeran and Katy Perry are just a couple examples of artists who have found themselves in legal hot water over their music.

-Goodwill-

The next aspect of music I want to talk about is goodwill. Music is art and art is put out there without any expectation of making money or anything like that. Art is meant to be communicative and to be shared with anyone who wants to hear it. Whenever you go to create your art, you shouldn't be thinking "what's something that's going to sell", it doesn't work like that.

You need to be open like the radio antenna receiving frequencies and let the music happen naturally. Your ear will help guide what will sound the best, and once the bones of a song are established, it will be a lot easier to fine tune it and add all the elements it needs to shine. Thinking ahead of time that you're just going to write a hit will only lead you to a lot of frustration.

There is footage of the pop artist Sia writing with a piano player and she's literally just belting out melodies and calling out chords to the pianist to go to really accentuate her melodies and match them perfectly. She would be singing and then just call out, "go to the 4", and then continue singing melodies before the next bar would come up, she would call out, "the six", and so on.

It's pretty impressive to see creativity naturally flow through someone like that and creating something that could be a hit but it's just scatting in beautiful melodies. This is what's its like to create a piece of art that just flows through you naturally. It's just creating and letting it flow.

Then when it comes to your lyrics, you want to think of something that will provide some goodwill to someones life. You want something they can relate to, even if the song was initially about a single moment in your life. It's how we tell the stories about what we've went through that can break through and touch someone else for something that happened similarly in their life.

Is it a wonder why there are so many love songs out there? People want to feel in love, and since a lot of people fall in love, there will probably be a ton of heartache associated with those times. That's why there are so many songs that do well that cater to that particular type of emotion because its something a lot of people are going through at any given time. What are some scenarios that you have seen people go through or have experienced yourself that you could turn into a song that gives peoples lives some goodwill? This will give you a great way to generate ideas that actually resonate with people.

-Profit-

Now when you provide goodwill and value to people, they will become fans of you. When people become fans of yours, they will want to support you and a lot of times that support can be financial in nature. This brings us to profit.

There are a lot of people out there that will help you have a stable music career. However, no music career can exist without profit. No matter what some snooty college professor may tell you or some weird forum on Reddit, you need profit and there is nothing wrong with seeking profit. You can very easily create something with genuine goodwill in mind and then figure out the ways to monetize that creation and the transaction is fair and enjoyed by all parties.

I've seen fans overpay for merchandise at our merch table and when we try to give them back their $50 in change they will tell us to keep it. We recently had a guy spend $215 dollars on probably $75 worth of merchandise simply because he wanted to support us. This was someone who had never seen a show before in his life, and actually showed up from an ad he saw on Facebook. That show by the way probably only had 18 people there, it was a pretty small place.

However, it doesn't matter the size of the venue when you know how to generate a good profit. I've sold thousands in bars and barely a hundred in a theatre gig, it just depends on the quality of the show and the quality of your sales process. Sales will be the engine running your business and making sure you have all your systems running smoothly.

Don't be afraid of sales, it's not like you're Billy Mayes doing some hard pitch on an infomercial late at night (no hate though, Billy sold millions). Sales is just simply uncovering the value of what you have to offer so well that it helps people make a decision. You may uncover the value and people may say "eh", but there will be people who are ready to make the decision to say "yes".

-Spontaneous-

Ideas that actually make you money in your music business will come spontaneously, just like ideas for songs or ideas for parts that will one day be in a song. I want to talk about being spontaneous in your art. Creativity is a very spontaneous type of thing, sometimes it takes a while for things to click, but once they do, we start taking massive action and our results explode.

There is, however, nothing worse than being in a situation where you have this amazing idea whether be lyrics or song ideas, and there is no way to capture it other than memory. Our brains are not equipped to hold multiple things at the front of our awareness, think of your mind at any given time like a stage. You can only have a certain amount of people on stage before there is no more room, and if you try to remember your idea through all the little daily tasks you'll have to complete before you can try the idea or map it out, you'll lose the idea every time.

-Systematic-

You need to have ways that you can capture your spontaneous moments of creative realization. This is where being systematic come in. Make sure to start getting more organized with your music business and all of the components that make it up. I recommend having this app one of my real estate mentors told me about called, Evernote. It's a great way to organize all the different things you've got going on in your life whether it's capturing musical ideas, writing down lyrics, or even personal obligations you've got going on that need checklists or whatever you need.

I remember when one of my favorite artists, Mark Tremonti, was telling a story about how he had a system to capture all his ideas. He went a bit old school and had this tape recorder that he would capture ideas on, and he would eventually fine tune the ideas to get them up to shape and put them on his laptop.

So the combination of a tape recorder and a laptop were where all his ideas he had been accumulating for 10 years or so was on those two different devices. Unfortunately, one night Mark had his backpack stolen which contained both his tape recorder and his laptop along with all the different ideas that were on it were gone forever.

This is about as frustrating as it can get as an artist because you don't have all those different ideas at the front of your brain at all times. Like I mentioned earlier, there is only so much data we can hold in our head at one time. So how do we learn from this experience?

We would be wise to upload our musical ideas to a 3rd party app or software that will hold all of the ideas, and if someone stole all the devices in your house, you will still have all your ideas safe and sound. My system is very simple and easy to access for most people out there.

Whenever I have an idea, I pull up the voice memo app on my iPhone, then I upload that file to Evernote to have a copy that is independent of my Apple device. I can pull up that idea on any device I want by typing in my username and password. Having a system like this will give you peace of mind to ensure that no matter what, your ideas are protected and archived properly.

-Collaboration-

One of the last traits I want to bring up for the art side of this yin yang concept that we've been talking about, is collaboration. A lot of other artists or people have resources that you don't. Instead of us viewing competitively, we would be better off in most cases to figure out how to develop a strategic relationship that allows you to leverage other peoples resources. This is one of the most important aspects of being a resourceful entrepreneur.

You might want to reach out to other bands to see if there is a collaboration you can come up with for a show, a feature in one of your songs, or even a way you can market or advertise together to make one of the previous two examples do better when it's released. When you get someone's own self-interest intertwined with a project you're involved with, you're going to have a better partner in your collaboration.

Sometimes, collaboration may come at a hefty price tag, but if you have a strategy and execute properly, it could be a winning strategy. For instance, your dream fans may be following someone who is pretty influential in your scene. You may find a way to pay them for their time so they will work with you. It's a nice quick way to get some decent attraction to what you've got going on, but it is definitely not cheap.

There is a concept created by a guy named Chet Holmes, called the Dream 100. I want you to list out 100 (or as many as you can) influencers that have your dream audience. Now you can start actively trying to follow what these people are doing to see how you could provide value to what they're doing, and earning your way into their ecosystem.

-Competition-

Now while you will have your dream 100 and all the people who will be your peers, we have to recognize that we are still in business, and business is a competition. Now competition can be friendly, even if it is intense. I'm not saying that you compete with your dream 100, but compete with the people who are in your immediate space or at your current level.

There are tons of bands that have zero talent or business being on stage that will take opportunities away from you because they're more competitive than you and are playing the game while you might be on the sidelines. It's time to start getting a bit of a fire and start to do things to become the best in your area.

You don't have to start being unfriendly or rude to anyone, just start executing. Execute with the idea that you're going to beat everyone by competing with yourself so well, that it propels you forward to be better. Let's be honest, there are only a certain amount of slots on the bill of that show, festival, or whatever. Time to start doing the work to ensure that it's you!

Both of the sides of art and entrepreneurship need to be integrated in to your music business and balanced in a way that creates harmony. You need to be able to balance your business with your art and your art with your business. That may sound like nonsense to you, but I can assure you it's far from it.

You need to be able to put on your musician hat and create art that will impact and reach millions, but still keep in mind your an entrepreneur that needs to profit in order to sustain and grow in order to continue to create more art.

Conversely, you need to be able to make efficient business decisions like a skilled, trained entrepreneur while also remembering that at the end of the day you're an artist pursuing their passion with a skill that brings joy and unity to masses of people.

Whenever you're doing activities that are primarily business or art related, you will need to be able to act efficiently within that role without becoming too unbalanced or one-sided. Whenever you're inside the studio recording, you need to be focused and immersed into your art.

However, if you don't organize your day effectively like an entrepreneur, you could waste hundreds or thousands of dollars wasting time in the studio on things that won't get your song to sound any better or get your recording done faster. If you're in a meeting with your manager or a label you want to make sure you put deals together that will be profitable, but not at the cost of the authenticity or expression of your art.

Our ability to achieve something is in direct proportion to our ability to maintain focus on it. If we are to achieve balance in both our business and our art, we need to begin to focus on all the subtleties and nuances of being a professional musician. We will break these strategies into the two frameworks I mentioned earlier: balancing business with art and balancing art with business.

Each will require a focused and specified approach to handle the issues you will encounter when attempting to balance both of these aspects of your life. Let's dive a little deeper into these balancing acts and see the different roadblocks and pitfalls you need to avoid to achieve balance.

Balancing Business with Art

"It's not about the money, it's about serving for the sake of serving without expectation. The money comes when you stop chasing it."
—Daxton Page

This Is The Business Inside Of The Art

Too many musicians have either A) not been given the proper knowledge or the efficient tools they'll need to actually start a business and make a profit while doing so and doing so with the highest integrity. B) swept up in ideologies that have attached some dirty meaning to money and that if you pursue profit of any kind that you're some sort of exploiter or oppressor. The former comes from a lack of education about money in America's public school system, but more broadly government backed education as a whole. Which if you think about it at first, it really doesn't make much sense on the surface.

You'd think the government would want to educate people to make as much money as they can so they could get them in higher tax brackets and inevitably make more tax money. Then you realize how the most successful entrepreneurs limit their tax burden, legally, and it starts to make sense why they don't teach it. The tax code allows for these deductions and if everyone knew it, that's less revenue for the government.

As a result of this complicated and often very convoluted system, most musicians (being creative types) avoid this subject almost entirely and dive completely into their musical and creative side. Now, there is utility in emersion and radical imbalance for a short period of time, but often musicians are so emerged in the art side that they completely ignore, and therefore, poorly understand the broader game of money and business. You need to understand your craft, but at a certain point you need to make the commitment to become a professional artist and not just a hobbyist (if that is your dream).

I remember this one artist I worked with in Oklahoma way back in the day, and he was one of those people who never wrote music but was really good at learning other peoples music. He was an incredibly talented player, but every time he tried to form a band it would always disintegrate.

His projects would do this because when it really came down to brass tax, he was just a hobbyist. He was obsessed with music on a deep level but was more excited about the idea of his ego being lifted by being a professional than he was actually dedicated to learning the strategies and tactics of professionals so he could have success.

Hobbyists are stuck in "the dream", and that's okay for them. They really wouldn't care if their music reached the masses or made an impact, they'd only want success that came easy to them and had the potential to raise their status. That way they can lord it over all the other hobbyists who didn't get to do what they did, but if you compared their merits to a professional it would be laughable.

If you feel no need or rush to make a name for yourself, and you're completely content just playing in your bedroom or garage and never take your playing online, to the stage, or never make a living off your music, then you need to be honest with yourself about that.

There is nothing wrong with being a hobbyist, but there is a problem when a hobbyist starts to enter the professional domain and not take it seriously because they just want a taste of the social capital artists get. You have to know what you truly want from your life, and don't tell yourself stories that you're not going to embody. That will create cognitive dissonance and make you start to not enjoy the art that gave you so much joy and fulfillment.

So how do we begin to balance the business side of the music industry into our lives and not have it negatively impact our art? We need to address some underlying fears that people have about integrating business into their artistic process because they feel it will hurt the quality of their art. Fear is where a lot of problems are for most people, I've talked to people who are trying to start businesses and they worry about the littlest things possible because they're so scared of the uncertainty of taking a risk on something.

Let's dive into the core fears people have around becoming a professional and how you can start to overcome these fears. Though the ancient greek philosopher Seneca once said "we often suffer more in imagination than in reality", I kinda prefer it the way Bobby McFerrin said it, "don't worry, be happy." Time to learn how to master fear!

Let's go!

Facing & Conquering Your Fear

The first fear we need to address is the fear is the fear of failure. A lot of people are scared to implement business into their lives because they're scared of what happens when they fail at something.

Notice I said "when" and not "if", because you're not to going to escape failure, all of the most successful people in every field will tell you that failure if learned from is essential. You and I must learn to fail well, so that when we get punched, we get back up and learn how to dodge it next time.

If you don't have the bad show, you don't know what you can do to make a good show. If you don't feel what its like to play a gig where no one shows up, you won't appreciate what it took to get people to the gig. Now don't get me wrong, one of the best strategies is to learn from other peoples mistakes and not have to make them for yourself, which is one of the purposes of this book.

However, the fear of failing will slow you down and possibly prevent you from puling the trigger on really good opportunities because you're scared as to what could happen if you don't pull it off.

One of the fears that is attached to this fear of failure is the fear of judgement. What happens if we try to do something cool to us? People are going to make remarks and judge us, and if we fail, they're going to judge us more. That social pressure can feel like a lot especially once you build up to thousands of fans, but I want to impart some wisdom that I was taught a long time ago.

No one who has ever lived on this planet, who has ever done ANYTHING of value has ever did so without haters. There's a difference between critics and haters, critics like you and want you to be better and haters want to do nothing but bring you down. Ignore your haters, the only value they have to you is a sign that you are on the right path to actually doing something worth a damn.

Fear is natural and evolutionarily programmed, there is a reason your brain feels that emotion and there is utility in that. The problem really comes when we become afraid to feel the fear and learn how to use and embrace it. The philosopher Alan Watts once said, "when you can really allow yourself to be afraid and you don't resist the experience of fear, you are truly beginning to master fear. But when you refuse to be afraid you are resisting fear, and simply that sets up the vicious cycle of being afraid of fear, and being afraid of being afraid of fear."

These wise words outline a problem of people's inability to embrace fear and use it, but instead they are used by fear and fear jumps into the drivers seat, making most of the decisions. Artists are very sensitive to fear, especially when you're high in neuroticism (the Big 5 personality trait) like I am.

You can't let fear rule your life, fear is a tool to be used for you. Let me give you an example of using fear: I remember being about 40 lbs overweight for my size, which isn't a crazy amount of being overweight, but I felt lethargic all the time. I didn't feel like I had any energy and I didn't like how I looked.

Now what do most people do in this very common situation? They fantasize about what it will look like when they've got six-pack abs and big biceps because they think that will get them in the gym, but that's actually the worst way to motivate yourself to take action.

Guess what I used that led to me losing 60lbs within a year just eating a very healthy salad everyday for lunch, never lifting a single weight? Fear. I told myself, "Dax, if you don't lose weight and start treating your body with more respect, you could potentially die of a heart attack when you're 45, heart problems run in your family, your wife will be devastated and if you have kids you're going to leave them fatherless", kind of morbid right?

I bet some of you felt uncomfortable just reading that. Good. What do you think happened when I had those days where I thought "ehh I'm tired of this salad", I remembered the fear of not being healthy and the consequences of my actions if I failed.

Do you think I ate the salad those days? Damn right I did, I would choke that thing down if I had to. My vitals were great, BMI (Body Mass Index) was looking good, felt great, looked great (in my opinion), and sure enough...the haters came in.

Surprisingly to me, some were even my family. My doctors were very happy with my transformation, but my haters said I looked sick. Ironic right? That is a perfect analogy for how it will be in this business sometimes.

You will start to make art that means a lot to you and you will push yourself into new exciting territories and people will call you a sell-out. That's just how it works, but the point is that you don't have to let fear lock you up and prevent you from taking actions or making decisions, they can be great tools for motivation. Make fear wind in your sails, pushing you where you need to go even when it seems easy to quit.

The last fear we need to talk about is a big one, and it's the fear of more money. Finish the sentence, more money more _____? Did you say problems? If so, that's one example of culture conditioning a feeling or association to gaining wealth. The real answer is more money more *freedom*! They don't tell you that the problems you have when you are wealthy are WAY better problems to have than when you're broke. One of my mentors shared this wisdom,

"If you set a thermostat on your air conditioning system to 72 degrees, and the temperature in the air is below 72 it will not click on. As soon as the air temperature goes above 72, the AC kicks on and works to bring it back down to 72 degrees. When it comes to the fear of more money, people tend to have this in reverse.

Most people have a number in their mind pertaining to the cost of their housing, their car, their food; the amount of money needed to be able to survive per a year. They may not be happy with the number but they know that if they at least make that much they will be ok. So when they reach the amount in their head, they tend to stop or slow down."

Researches at IBM took people that were making $40,000 a year that had complained they were overworked and underpaid and gave them each a $10,000 raise. They expected people to work harder because they were getting paid more. Many of these people had the 40,000 mentality so when the money went up to $50,000 they worked 15% less. This study proves just how big of a problem the fear of more money can be. Let's get one thing straight, profit is good.

Profit is to be invested back into the business so the fans can have the best experience possible, and at the same time allowing you to live more comfortably so that you can be free to create your art without all the typical financial concerns a lot of people, and most definitely professional musicians, have.

Trick Your Money Thermometer

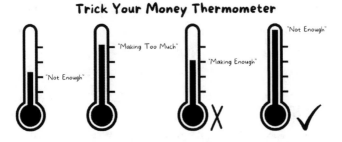

Imagine what that would be like to have all your financial needs met and you were just free to create your art all day without stress about bills or expenses. How would that make you feel? How much more creative could you be? How much more time could you dedicate back into your art so that it's as best as it can possibly be? All these questions are supposed to get you to see what's possible when you balance your business into your art properly.

When you've got your money right, you are free to create more art and not be incentivized to make stale art for the sole reason of profit "just to keep up". If you set up your profit centers right, you're not relying on your music specifically to keep things going, and you can free up that space in your mind to just focus on art when it comes down to creating it.

How To Sell As A Musician

I had this fan message me on social media one time, and she was asking me about the different ways that a fan could support an artist. She was listening on her favorite streaming platform, but she didn't feel like her engagement was resulting in enough benefit for the artists she loved. A lot of your fans are in this dilemma.

They want to support you more, but a lot of artists and bands only offer a minimal amount of vehicles from which the fans can support them. They'll offer music on streaming, merchandise, and that's usually it for about 90% of artists. So in the absence of multiple valuable ways to support, fans don't. They'll continue to stick to routine, and you will not be able to grow and give the fans what they want.

The fans either want more music, more music videos, more social media content, more shows, more merchandise, more opportunities for 1-on-1 meet & greets, or more exclusive content. Which means you need to find more ways to provide those things of value to your fans, and give them the most valuable way to support as possible. This means inevitably, you will have to learn not only about marketing but also selling, or put another way, you will need to learn attraction and persuasion.

This is what a good portion of musicians are scared of when they begin to implement sales processes in their music business, however. They're worried that if they begin to ask their fans for money that they will turn people away out of offense of being sold something, or they are afraid they will come across and unauthentic, like a used-car salesmen or cheesy infomercial host.

While I see where these fears come from, they're mostly exaggerated and let me explain why. As long as you don't try and be someone you're not, you have nothing to fear as far as being viewed as some cheesy salesperson. You see, you're in a unique predicament when it comes to business, you're an artist. You don't have to sell fans as hard on liking you because they already like you for the most part.

It's easier for an artist to influence their fans to give them their phone or email than it is for some business to get the public to give them their phone or email. You're somewhat in a position of authority in the psychology of your audience.

Don't let this go to your head, because it's very easy to happen when you get surrounded with people who are constantly complimenting you and peanut buttering you up for something.

Now, while you want to be authentic, you need to sound enthusiastic about whatever it is you're selling. This is where people feel weird, but let me help. If you talk like how you normally talk to your friends to a mass of people, you're going to come across as boring.

So what I'd recommend is to get sold on yourself…Wait, what? Yeah, what you should do is realize the value you actually have and start to become excited about providing more value to your fans. I remember when I was very first trying to figure out this whole music business thing, I was in a little school for kids who wanted to learn how to form a band. It was called the Oklahoma Rock Academy, cute right? A bunch of 12-16 year olds get together to learn songs together and play shows to get used to being in a rock band. Sound like a great idea right? Well, while I thought the concept was cool, it was definitely lacking in execution on a few fronts. One being that the songs we were learning to get started were all top 40 songs by the likes of Katy Perry, Adele, Kelly Clarkson, and thank goodness one Neil Young song. While I have nothing against these artists, I didn't want to perform their music (certainly not in a "rock" academy).

I wasn't the only person who felt like this in the group. You see being a rock vocalist is hard, so there are very few who are trained and seasoned enough to hop on a stage and start belting out high notes or screams without working on it for a good amount of time. So the vocalists that signed up just happened to be female vocalists who didn't listen to rock at all. Now don't get me wrong, there are some amazing female rock and metal vocalists out there, but if you don't get rock singers for rock groups, it's never going to sound great. So because we had pop female singers our setlist was very limited.

Not to mention of the two female singers we had, one was older but very religious, and her family would object to her performing any songs that would fall under rock. "Crazy Train" by Ozzy was "right out" apparently, so I knew that the other heavier material we all wanted to play was probably never going to happen.

As a result of all of this, no one in the band (outside the singers) was happy about performing a local "grand opening/reveal" show playing a setlist of top 40 songs, when none of us listened to pop regularly. How do you think our energy on stage made the audience feel? Probably pity because we looked like we really didn't want to be there for the most part. We would just look down and play the songs while focusing on our parts.

I tried to smile and look like I was enjoying performing "Hot & Cold" by Katy Perry, I was not sold on what we were doing. No one was sold, and frankly neither was anyone in the audience. The people that weren't parents that came to check out the academy had left by the time the set was finished. Sucks for them because we got jam solos to "Canon in D" for our closer. I actually had fun on that one because I could cut loose.

Since I wasn't sold on the academy much anymore, I just did the bare minimum to get by and eventually left the academy to pursue something I *was* sold on. It just goes to show you, you can't have confidence and success in anything you aren't sold on.

I want you to think about how excited you would be if the product/service you are about to sell to your fans, was actually being sold *to* you by your favorite artist or a band you like. How excited would you be? Now transfer the excitement you have about the idea of receiving that value from your favorite artist, and turn it into enthusiasm for what you're providing for your fans.

You need to think "even if it's uncomfortable for me to admit, I'm someones favorite artist. And if I would love this from my favorite artist, my fans would love to receive this from me". The only thing holding you back from that point is doubt and uncertainty about the value you are providing. In those moments of doubt, just ask your self the question I mentioned earlier.

Would you enjoy this deal or item if your favorite artist made an offer for it? If so, then be excited about providing that opportunity to your fans. Your fans cannot support you if they have no vehicle or opportunity to do so.

One of the best ways I know to give your fans a vehicle to support you is to create "offers" using sales funnels. An offer, simply put, is a bundle of valuable items and services. The bundling of these valuable and unique items increases the value of your offer, which increases what price you can charge for the offer. If your offers value is bigger than your price your fans will buy every time, and they'll be happy because they got something so much cooler in return.

You must find a price point that is not only profitable but genuinely good value for the fans. Artists make the mistake of viewing this too much from the perspective on an artist and not enough from the perspective of a fan. Think of what would be valuable first, then build the offer around it.

When it you get down to it, you really have two things you can offer your fans: tangibles and intangibles. Tangibles are things like merchandise, and intangibles are things like meet & greets.

Tangible offers have something you would call "retail value", these are price points based on what you would pay for these type of items out in a retail space. These items have pretty fixed price points or price ranges because there is already a precedent in the market place for what people are willing to pay for it. Use a bottle of water as an example!

If you were to try and buy a water bottle from the grocery or convenient store, how much would you pay for a bottle of water? Probably $1 to $2 in that context, right? Well, what if you were at the airport or a live event? Now you'll probably pay $2 to $4 for the same exact product! Why is that?

A lot of retail price is determined off of the context, scarcity, and demand for that particular product. If you're at a concert, shirts can be actually anywhere from $25 at a bar, all the way to $45 to $50! There will be designs that are only available for that tour which emphasizes something called "scarcity".

Scarcity drives the price up quicker than any other economic force out there. So if you're selling something online is "mass" quantity, there's not a lot of scarcity in that. However, if you've only bought a limited amount of this new design so you need to get one now before we run out, introduces a bit more scarcity and makes people's desire to buy go up. So if you want to make money with tangibles, you need to take advantage of these different persuasion techniques.

Intangible offers are things like soundcheck access, meet & greets, etc. These type of items do not have a retail price, counter to what a lot of people think. You may see musicians in your particular genre doing VIPs and they all may share a price range, let's say for instance that the average is anywhere from $75 - $150. The reason you may be seeing that is based on either: a) they're just following their guts, b) they are just copying what other people are doing, and therefore, charging the same, and c) are afraid to charge more because they don't feel worth it, or that fans will pay.

Understanding Value

All of those concerns crumble under one rule, perceived value. There is flexibility and variation in price based on the perceived value of the artist. A meet & greet with Beyonce is probably worth a lot more than a meet & greet of your favorite local, regional, or even national artist. In fact, the last time Beyonce and Jay-Z went out and had VIP packages, the most expensive offer was $1991 and the cheapest offer was $391. You might be thinking, "Dax, what on earth could be in an offer that is worth two grand?".

Well let me tell you, this "Runway VIP Experience" contained: one ticket up on the runway so you will be right in front of Beyonce while she performs and will probably get caught on camera is she shoots any b-roll, an intimate backstage tour, VIP parking, VIP lounge & bar access, pre-show private merch shopping, VIP gift item, VIP hosts and concierge, interactive games and cell phone charging stations, and the last thing I'll include (because there is more) is a VIP lounge laminate. Wow, right?!

That's a whole bunch of stuff that you're getting, and on top of it, you get the best view of Beyonce out of everyone else at the show. This level of intimacy, exclusivity, and extravagance pushes the value to way over $10,000 for stars like Beyonce and Jay-Z, however, they only charge 20% of that value which would be about $2,000.

What you need to figure out is how you can increase the value proposition of your offer so that you can provide for your fans the most intense, amazing experience possible. Once you do that, you will hopefully have increased the value to such an extent that the price seems like a great deal regardless of how high it is because the value is so *much* higher.

Remember to use what you would enjoy from your favorite artists to create offers for your audience. Some musicians may say things like "well I'm not as big as *(insert artist)*, I can't offer that service and certainly not at that price". The answer is: it depends.

Some artists are just now starting out, and that means inevitably, you can't charge as much as Beyonce. However, that doesn't mean you can't provide the offer for a price that matches the perceived value of you or your band.

There are also multiple tiers of value inside of a concert ticket (or anything for that matter). This is called a value ladder, a term popularized by Russell Brunson. A value ladder is when you have a tier of products or services that increase in value (and by consequence increase in price).

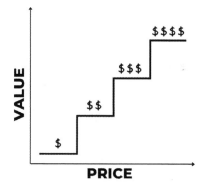

For instance, you have a value ladder based on location to the stage. GA tickets, Gold tickets, and Platinum tickets. However, you can also have a value ladder based on VIP experiences. You have VIP tickets, Gold VIP tickets, and Platinum VIP tickets. If you go to any of the big acts that sell out arenas and have VIP ticket packages, you will see this.

Guitarist Steve Vai, even has a tier of VIP tickets where you can get a guitar! It starts with a VIP merch package where you get a whole bunch of merch, some commemorative items related to the tour, VIP venue entry, and a ticket to the show.

Then you move up to the next step in this value ladder, and you get a meet and greet package plus soundcheck access, as well as all the previous tiers items. Except the tour poster gets autographed with this package. Not to mention a bonus pre-show Q&A with Steve. Starting to provide a lot of value, right?

Now we move to the next tier where you get everything I just mentioned plus a guided tour of Steve's instruments and gear as well as a front row ticket to the show. That's a full-on experience if I've ever heard of one! Finally, we move to the last tier where you get everything I just mentioned plus an Ibanez Jem Jr. guitar plus a signed custom pick-guard!

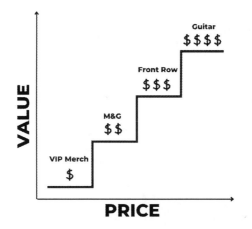

When should you start to add meet & greets to your shows? When you have enough fans that are die-hard enough to buy it. When do I start a fan club? As soon as possible, this one can be done. By anybody at any stage in their career.

You see there is a bit of variance to how these strategies are implemented, but overall the motto is the same. "If you want success, model success", that's a loose Tony Robbins quote, but it's as close to signal as I can get on the subject.

If you see a cool behind the scenes offer or something from your favorite artist or band, screenshot it or find a way to archive it as a potential strategy that you will do in your own unique, improved way. If you see artists offering 1-on-1 lessons, start seeing if anyone in the band can teach an instrument. If you see artists start including something cool in their VIP, you include something just like it in your VIP.

By modeling success, you may not be able to charge what they charge, but you can improve your own value proposition so much that everyone around you's VIP looks bland in comparison to yours!

When you can position yourself as the one with the BEST service, or the BEST VIP, no one has a problem paying for a premium because they know they're getting a premium offer. Now I know people are going to be reading this and thinking, "but Dax! Won't these higher prices alienate my fans that can't afford it?", and the answer is, potentially but not always!

You will have fans who paid for your VIP because they saw they were getting a great deal because you were undercharging for a great VIP. Once you raise your prices you will be stating you have more value to provide, and people who could afford to pay more will happily pay more because you're providing more value.

However, some of the fans that are, let's be nice and call them, frugal, will be turned off by the higher price. You can provide a tiered VIP package where there is a economic option and a premium option if you really want to include them. However, there are times where you may not want to do that.

Protecting Your Highest Levels of Value

There are some customers that exist out there who will look for the absolute cheapest thing they possibly can, they'll always complain about prices, they're always looking for a discount or something for free, they want the most from the band for having given the least above people who have given the most to the band, and so on and so forth.

I saw someone look me dead in the face and said I was robbing him for making money off a Koozie, and then proceeded to accost me at the merch table. You remember koozie's, the foam can and bottle holders that keep your hand from freezing while you're drinking all night? Yeah over one of those. We were in Cleveland, OH and we were at this venue that was right outside from a beautiful bridge with wonderful scenery around it.

We however, were playing in a place that resembled more of an open warehouse full of concert goers. There were 4 bands on the bill and we kicked off the show, and while it certainly wasn't the best show we had ever played, it wasn't the worst either. I do remember I went a little crazy on my guitar and opened a wound right under my pinky. It looked pretty gnarly and so after the set I had to run over to the restrooms to clean my hand off. No one wants to shake the guitar players bloody hands.

The merch was up by the front door where people come in, so after I washed up I started doing my normal job of running the merch table. Because the merch table was so far away from the stage, it was a really slow night. And when you have a slow night of merch for the headliners, the openers get kicked in the pants. If they don't have enough for the headliner, they sure as hell don't have enough for you.

So we're grinding trying to get some sales, and here comes this middle aged guy walking towards me with what I could only assume to whiskey or scotch. He was rocking back and forth a good amount so I could tell this guy had a great time so far, if you know what I mean.

He walks up and looks at our merchandise for about a minute. Then stumbles upon a koozie (obvious choice for him in retrospect), his eyebrows get tense and he begins to squint at our price sheet. He then released a borderline shout and said, "$5 for a fucking koozie?!"

I looked at him somewhat confused because of the hundreds of shows we had played up until that point, no one had ever complained about the price of a koozie. In fact, they were one of our most consistent sellers throughout the years. I told him, "well we've got to eat tonight and make it to the next gig", to which he responded, "oh sheesh, you guys are going to eat just fine". We didn't eat that night, but that's besides the point.

This was someone who was so cheap and so out to get a deal at the expense of any profit you need to make to get to the next show, that they were willing to spend I'm assuming $20 on alcohol but not $5 on a koozie. Then proceeds to basically say you're ripping him off because you wouldn't lose money on a koozie by taking it for $1.

You probably, do not want those people taking your VIPs because your VIPs are one of the most intimate, high-level parts of your value ladder as an artist, and you want to make sure you audit the community you are going to keep at this level.

If you bring in people like that to a laid back, close-nit group that you are trying to maintain, you may have people who come into your group who can cause other people to leave. There's a way you can enforce this to people who do have the money to pay for your premium VIPs but are still being obnoxious or jerks. You can have a clause that you reserve the right to end their VIP if they are behaving inappropriately towards other VIPs or to the process, however you'd like to define that.

I've heard many stories about people offering great products to people, and the customer will complain about a misspelled word in a free bonus product they sent to them for the price of postage. There are many misconceptions about who is willing to pay for what, and don't assume that by raising your prices you'll be alienating your fans to a point where they don't want to see you anymore. They want to come see you because of the connection that have to you through your music, and they will always show up for that regardless if they buy anything.

HOW TO RUN A SPLIT TEST

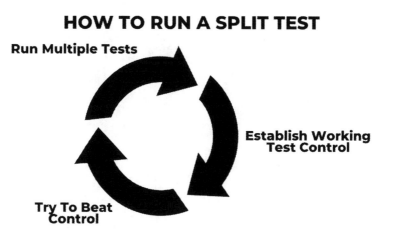

Run Multiple Tests

Establish Working Test Control

Try To Beat Control

All that being said, it's very important that you price test and run experiments to figure out who your die hard fans are, and how much you can charge without starting to lose money because everyone thinks it's too expensive and won't buy. If people halfway fill out a form and don't buy, hit them up and ask them why they didn't buy!

Ask them if it was the price and if there were some different prices you could offer if they would buy. It's all about serving the fan the best you can not assuming for them that you know what they're going to say or think about an offer. The only way to know for sure, is to get their contact info and ask them! Don't be shy, these are people who like your music and are potentially interested in supporting you by buying your merchandise.

When you have a fan-centric business model, you can feel good when you present an offer to your fans because you know you're doing this to bring them something they'll love. As opposed to a business-model predicating on using fans as just another means of money. We want to view our fans as both customers and people we want to serve, and that is how you make sure you never let the business outweigh the importance of looking out for your fans and giving them the best you have to offer.

Balancing Art with Business

"Show me the incentive, and I will
show you the outcome."
—*Charlie Munger*

This Is The Art
Inside Of The Business

Now down to business, literally. We've all seen this band I'm about to describe, so allow me to tell you a story about a band I went on tour with about half a decade ago. This is was one of our very first big tours that we had ever been on in our career up to that point, and when we kicked the first night off, we were pumped! It was a great night at The Music Factory in Battle Creek, MI, and we thought the headliner put on a dang good show.

We all went to the next stop and met up the next day at the venue. Everything is business as usual, which is a lot of hurrying up to wait 6 or more hours. Well the next show goes great as well, and then we hear the headliner go up and play the same set as the night before.

Now this isn't uncommon among traveling bands. You rehearse a set, and you go out and perform it every night and get better and better as you perform it. However, there was something a little bit different about the way this band did it, or should I say how their singer did it.

Every single night, he would say the exact same things. I'm not hating on the idea of having a loose collection of things you can say that you know works with a crowd because you've tested it over and over again to see what works. This singer however, would say exactly the same things to start the show, in between songs, during songs (outside of the actual lyrics obviously), after each song. The same jokes in the same order every single night for about a month and a half.

I tried to give them the benefit of the doubt, but we ended up going on tour with them about a year later, and they were still playing the exact same set. The same one we heard a year prior, jokes in all. We started to get really confused when we saw the first night on tour with them again that it was all exactly the same since the last time we saw them. We ended up walking over to their tech (who was a friend of ours) and asked him, "dude, is it just me or do they play the exact same set every show?", to which he responded, "nope. They've been playing this set since a little after I joined the crew and that was about 3 years ago.

They were so concerned about getting paid that they stopped pushing themselves creatively and ended up doing the exact same set with rare minor variations for literally 3 years. I'm not kidding even a little bit.

What kind of relationship do you think these band members had after doing that same set for so long? A very unstable one with constant fighting that was fueled by alcohol is what it ended up being. There were fights, knives pulled, guitars smashed, and it was just all around bad.

Every single person had their own way of maintaining the status they had once had, and you could see that what was once a beautiful connection to their art, had turned into a full fledged job that they punched in and out every day. Doing the exact same tasks with haunting similarity. The poor fans that they would play to twice in a years time would be treated to a lovely dose of the exact same show they had last time. This is what happens when you sacrifice authentic expression just to make a quick buck. Everything can become a tool of ego inflation. What happens is after we start to get momentum, we start to establish a certain level of certainty and comfort.

This comfort leads us to focus primarily on our economic necessities and can gradually lead us to forget about the purpose of art which is genuine, authentic expression. I'm not undermining the importance of keeping the debt and bill collectors away, but when you start to obsess about these things it can be easy to start to become unbalanced in your perspective.

These problems are really symptoms of poorly set up business systems. Most people fall into the trap of setting up their business systems around needing to invest more time in order to get more money. This sets up a predicament where in order to grow you need to sacrifice more of your time, and sometimes this can eat up all your free time.

Furthermore, even if you have all the free time in the world you will reach a point where your income will peak, and you will be out of time to invest. This is not a sustainable business model and can cause you to become cynical and start to sacrifice the quality of your art.

It is absolutely worth the investment to spend money to implement systems that will in return get you some of your time back. Having systems in place is the cornerstone of any successful business and will be one of the keys to giving you a solid income while allowing you to leave your art uncompromised.

Becoming Fan-Centric

Always remember, you make the most money whenever you provide the most value to your fans. The value exchange is a crucial concept, it's basically the cycle of how artists make money and how fans support them. If you break it down there are only 3 things that can be exchanges between an artist and their fans: time, capital, and emotion. If you set up your business systems around these exchanges, you will be given tremendous value from your fans.

Setting up systems around time effectively is where you have something that was once done manually that is now being converted into automation. Automation gives you your time back to create art.

An example would be hiring someone to run the merch table throughout the entirety of the show instead of you having to stand there the whole show before your set and immediately after which can give you very little downtime.

You can set up a system where you have your discounts and promotions scheduled on a calendar ahead of time so you don't have to keep track of all the different promotions you could do throughout the year. The whole point of systems are to get your time back so you can go back to creating the art that is exciting to you.

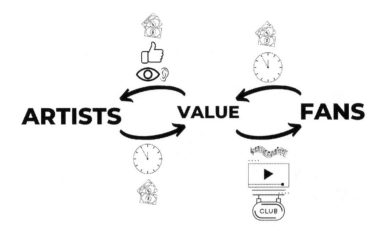

Systems usually require a bit of upfront work which will lead to the point where the system is ready to go and then only need maintenance from then on out. You want to think like an investor. If you invest your time, capital, and emotion into a great system, you will be setting up vehicles that improve your productivity. Which will allow you to have more time to create art or more capital to create more systems so you can automate again for growth.

One of the systems you need to set up properly is your sales process. This is where you're going to make your money. However, there is something crucial to understand whenever setting up your sales process. It's something that if you overlook, it will be very easy to lose balance between your business and your art, and that is the fans experience inside of your sales process.

Have you ever bought merch from a band? Doesn't it feel kind of distant from the artist? It's usually on a different website, it's just a bunch of items, you don't really see the band throughout the checkout process, or after you just supported them. It's usually some automated, template responses to your purchase. You just helped out a band you really enjoy and it feels more like checking out at JCPenny online.

I'm asserting that if you start to incorporate more a personalized and interactive sales process, that you will build rapport and trust with your fan-base and will potentially increase the frequency at which they purchase.

You may be thinking that creating a system sounds like a complicated mess right? Actually it's crazy simple. I have a little diagram that I've built to help you build systems inside you're business.

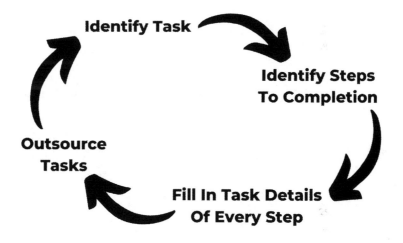

Steve Wynn, one of the people responsible for turning Las Vegas into the destination city it is and with a staggering net worth of $3.2B, has a famous story that exemplifies genuinely caring for your customers and turning them into die-hard fans.

The story goes that there was a bell hop named Ernesto Mendez, who was taking the bags of two elderly guests at the Wynn hotel up to their room, when once they arrived to their room the wife yells out, "Oh no! Honey, we left the medicine bag at home we're going to have to go home! You're a diabetic and we need those medications!". Ernesto asked the lady, "where do you both live?", to which she responded "We live in Woodland Hills, CA". Ernesto responded, "I have a brother in Encino, let me give him a call and see if he can drive over there and get your medicine bag for you. When do you need your medication?", and the lady responded, "we need it by 7:00am tomorrow".

Ernesto told his manager and drove all the way to Encino to his brother and back, arriving back in Vegas by about 4:00am getting the medicine bag to the front desk and instructed them to send the medicine to their room. Now that is the kind of love you should have for your fans and willingness to make sure whenever they go to one of your events, meet you in person, or go through on of your sales processes that they feel that welcomed, taken care of, and understood.

An additional benefit to genuine value is curiosity. If I went through a process to buy a shirt and there were all these interactive videos or pictures, I may even go through another one just to see what other kind of offers you've got.

You should also make things very simple and clear for your fans so they can effortlessly go through your process and feel like they just went through an *experience* more than a sales process.

Though profit will allow you to live comfortably and grow, remember that behind every sale is a human being. When you're always looking at things from the perspective of your fans, you're more likely to set up systems that actually give people value and build rapport with your fans.

One of the deadly traps of business is when people start to look at numbers so much and are so focused on growing those numbers that we forget behind all of the numbers are real people. This will not hurt your business, if anything it will help your business because when people feel understood and listened too, they are more likely to become die-hard fans.

You need to figure out how many different ways you can transfer the focus of a given activity from being about you to being about them, your fans. Then you'll start to see the engagement with your activities start to grow to massive numbers.

A lot of times artists delude themselves into thinking what they're really doing for themselves is somehow for the fans. If your stage show is designed and orchestrated to make everyone in the band's ego to be inflated, then people will find your show very egotistical and self-centered. Long story short, they won't connect with you.

However, if you design your show to connect with people and provide a show to them (that you would be blown away by if you were in the audience), people will respond to your shows.

The Secret Power Of Music

One of the greatest powers, if you want to call it that, that music has is the ability to raise peoples confidence and actually transform their lives. If you can create an experience that will help people grow in a community-like environment of something like a concert, people will feel a deep connection with your art and actually have the potential to change their lives for the better.

This is something that mainstream music will harnesses often, however, in a very cynical or profit-seeking manner. In my opinion, this can border on manipulation in the right context. Which is why I mentioned in the beginning of this that "with great power comes great responsibility", because when you create music that is designed to enable the worst parts of peoples behavior, intent starts to become irrelevant in relationship to the outcome of interpretation.

This is a fine-line, balancing act that is often very difficult to escape. On one side you have the artists saying, "let me create whatever I damn well please, I can't control how people use my music".

While on the other hand there is "you should be held responsible for people who used your music as fuel or inspiration for whatever crimes they commit against others or themselves". Interpretation is where art gets its subjectivity. The old saying "do as I say not as I do", never seems to work out however.

There was a hard rock, grunge band in the 90's named Alice In Chains, who's lead singer Layne Staley had a very public battle with heroin. Their songs lyrics were pretty evident of the singers struggles.

However, as honest as the lyrics were, some of that honesty bordered on glorification. Inevitably while they were at a show, a fan walked by them at a merch booth pointing to his arms (signifying he had just shot up some heroin, just like his hero). Jerry (their guitarist) and Layne said in an interview telling this story, that they never wanted the music to be seen as glorifying drugs.

However, because of Laynes carelessness in formulating of his pain, he inevitably enabled the really impressionable people in his audience to take hard drugs. Especially those who were going through significant struggles in their life which would lead them to be attracted to that kind of escapism in the first place.

Layne is not completely to blame for this because individuals are still responsible for their own actions, those kids decided out of their own free will to shoot up. However, to deny that Layne's words played a role in filtering their decision-making process, is dishonest.

> *"You can hypnotize people with the music and when you get them at their weakest point, you can preach into the subconscious what you want to say."*
> —Jimi Hendrix

This is the power that music has. It can influence or enable either the best sides of our behavior or the worst sides of our behavior. It is my belief that you must take a very good look at any songs that might particularly be misused for these types of destructive behaviors for your audience.

Sometimes you have to be brutally honest about something tough like addiction, but at least give a silver-lining of some kind, even if it's subtle. We are all striving for something better in our own lives, it's a human universal. In the end however, you are free to create what you desire. I just hope you understand the impact that poorly articulated lyrics about things of great severity such as addiction can have.

Be responsible, because with every freedom to do something has an equal importance of responsibility to uphold that freedom to the highest standards you can manage.

This is NOT to suggest that all your music always has to be serious and no fun. It's just a warning of what can happen when people don't think about the impact of different interpretations of their music. All of what I'm describing comes down to taking a moment to consider how what you're doing will impact your fans.

It doesn't matter whether it is your sales processes, your songwriting and arranging, or your shows. You'd be surprised how well your business will do when you aren't only considering things from your perspective, but also the people that will be experiencing your business.

This is one of the fundamental failures most people make in the business world generally speaking, they are so wrapped up in making the money that they don't focus on making something worth paying for. When you're only focused on how to make the money, you start to fall into traps of "success at all costs" mentalities, and by that I don't mean making meaningful sacrifices to make your music business work, I mean those who lie, cheat, and steal to make a quick buck.

When you focus on how you can provide something of value that someone would actually want to pay for it, the money comes easier and in more gratifying amounts. It will be because people feel like they received something of value rather than manipulated into buying something they didn't need nor want.

When your business starts to do well, you're going to have days where you make a lot of money. One thing that is essential for you to understand is that the best businesses are run by owners who invest their earnings back into the company, not by owners who use their companies earnings as a personal ATM.

What that means is that you want to take a good portion of the earnings you get and reinvest them back into fan experiences, songs, videos, show elements, etc. Flashing fancy clothes, expensive watches, or luxury cars is not going to give your fans that feeling of connection. It's purely posturing to do this.

Now, if you're able to make enough profit that you can reinvest back into the fans and have enough money left over for some more material things, then that's fine. That is considering your personal finances are taken care of first and foremost. This will ensure that you are laying the foundation for stable growth.

If you spend all your left over profit on yourself, then you have to sell more to fans before you can give them something of value. All because you spent all the money that could've been reinvested back in them on yourself, this is setting up the system that I mentioned in the beginning of this chapter.

The bands that have established a certain lifestyle based on earnings, then they have to go tour again to make enough money to stay out of debt (if they don't have any debt from their label), then spend it all maintaining their lifestyle, and inevitably the fans get little to nothing.

This is not about charity, this is about setting up business systems that will give your potential or existing fans an experience so valuable that they become a life-long fan. That will in turn grow your business and grow your profit, but more importantly it will grow your fan loyalty.

Your fans loyalty is one of the greatest assets your music business can have. If you have people that will support you via whatever vehicle you put in front of them (recorded music, merchandise, VIP upgrades, etc.), then you have someone who will support you financially to create the art you love to create for a lifetime.

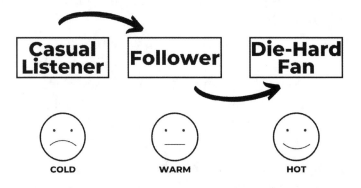

Listeners come and go, die hard fans usually don't go anywhere unless they're neglected, mistreated, or do not agree with a radical stylistic shift that you've made. However, if you've made a name for yourself because you're known for how much you give to your fans how you give to your community, how incredible it is to experience your events, you're more likely to keep fans and convert new ones.

One of Your Biggest Assets

....

Speaking of assets, your creativity is one of the most overlooked assets in your business. I don't understand why some of the most creative people on the planet will stiffen up and not use their creativity to improve their business. It's almost like musicians feel like when you're talking about business that everything has to be "all about business" and just a stale conversation about profit margins and sales processes.

Your creativity is actually the tool most valuable to your business to not only establish cool opportunities to get fans to support but also put together experiences that will separate you from the rest of your competition. I want to tell you about a band that used their creativity very well to demonstrate what I'm talking about.

There's a band from San Antonio, TX named Nothing More, and they have probably one of the most engaging and entertaining live shows in the hard rock genre since Rammstein. These gentlemen developed a section of their live show named the "Bassonator", where they roll out this contraption that locks a bass guitar in place to a swinging harness.

This harness is locked and unlocked depending on what position they want the bass to be in, and they'll just swing it in a 360 degree loop until they want to stop it at a certain position. In the beginning the bass player and guitar player play on this one bass guitar together, creating a very interesting arrangement.

Then, to add more excitement, the singer hops up to the top of this contraption and starts to drum on the strings with some drum sticks while the bass and guitar player hold the frets and create chords and melodies. All the while, the drummer is keeping the pace going with a perfectly orchestrated pulsing drum beat.

This performance was something that took me from a casual listener to a raging fan over-night, it was that fast. I actually didn't like Nothing More when I first heard them, I was kind of a rock purist at the time so I wasn't open to rock with electronic effects and production value. However, I was instantly sold when I was presented with an innovative performance that was masterfully executed. That wasn't the only type of performance enhancer of the night, there were a couple.

The point is that you can use your creativity to take a normal business conversation and turn it into a conversation where you come up with your next big idea. Don't become a strict number cruncher, you're a musician.

Use that creativity to your advantage to help take your business to the next level. This is where managers and outside, non-creative types can come in and start to stunt the conversation. If you allow yourself to have an open mind and not look at problems like problems, but look at them like opportunities, you will start to see the right way forward.

Who Moved My Cheese?

When COVID-19 started to take the stage worldwide, most people retreated into their homes and basically admitted defeat. I remember talking to our booking agent Evan and he was telling me how frustrated he was that all of his clients, big and small, were sitting on their hands and not trying to adapt to the marketplace. He was happy with us because we used the opportunity of COVID-19 (not the problem) to do lots of live stream performances, write more music, and build more business systems.

The only way we would have taken action on any of those things was if we weren't making decisions from a position of fear, but instead a position of opportunity or even abundance. This mindset allowed us to continue to grow while most stagnated or even lost momentum.

We got hate from people that thought we were being irresponsible. We even had one guy go on this huge rant on our page about how someone could track in COVID and pass it to the dogs and then the dogs would hop up on our pillows and we'd get infected that way.

We understood all the risks involved with our decisions, we also took precautions if someone wasn't feeling well. There was always open and honest communication, something every group should have.

There were even a couple weeks where we had to take off because a couple of members contracted COVID-19, they ended up being totally fine and we got back together when things were safer. While most people were inside watching too much news, we were in the trenches figuring out how to position and posture ourselves so that we could grow in our marketplace.

Think about when COVID-19 hit the world stage. We could've complained about show cancelations. We could have sat around waiting for the world to go back to normal. We could have sat on our hands and gave up on reaching out and providing value to our fans. Again, we did not do that and you shouldn't either.

Once we viewed the problem of COVID-19 as an opportunity, we started to do live streams that opened up a future vehicle of support for our fans that we had never tapped before. If we listened to the masses, we would have been no better or even worse off than before.

A lot of the problems you are going to face in this business are almost strictly mental in nature. Your psychology and mindset will, by-in-large, determine your success in any field. You can't beat someone who refuses to go down.

You can't stop someone who is always learning new ways to get things done. When one method ceases to work, you change the strategy but never change the goal. You keep your eyes locked in on the prize and narrow your action to get you where you want to go.

Creativity was the driving fuel that allowed us to grow and create the music and business systems we did, however, fear will kill your creativity. Remember our discussion on fear? You have to use fear instead of being used by it, and when your decisions are ruled by fear, it's easy to retract, withdraw, and lose your momentum. It's time to make decisions from a position of opportunity and abundance instead of fear.

I want to tell you about one of the most difficult challenges in my life that was saved by the use of creativity. It was November of the year 2017, and we had just gotten word that we were just accepted onto a tour with the band I mentioned previously, Nothing More, right after they were nominated for 3 Grammys.

This was one of the biggest opportunities the band had up to that point in our career and we were crazy excited. However, we had a huge problem. Our singer Jesse was struggling really bad with drug addiction. It had gotten to the point where he moved into my parent's house (which was where I lived and where our band headquarters were at the time), so that he could be around good influences and not alone with his urges.

One night, I had heard Jesse go into the garage and when I looked to see what was going on, I noticed the garage door was cracked a few feet. I looked underneath the garage door to see Jesse in the street next to a pickup truck. I never saw the exchange go down, but I confronted Jesse and asked what he was doing.

He lied and told me it was one pill he got to help with some shoulder injury he had, it was plausible at the time and so I let it go. I even felt bad for accosting him when he was trying to get sober. My mother and I found him the next morning almost dead from an overdose and he was very disoriented, ashamed, and angry. We had a talk with him, it was pretty futile. He was so out of it and frankly didn't want to hear any of it.

I was instructed to take him to work that day so we knew he actually went to work and didn't just go and get high again. Once I dropped him off, he immediately conned a relative into some money for a one-way plane ticket to Ohio (which was where his girlfriend lived at the time).

He called an Uber from work and left for Ohio, not telling anyone until he was gone and unreachable. We had one of the biggest tours of our entire career in literally a month and a half, and our singer was now no longer going to be able to rehearse hundreds of miles away. At this point, we could see that venues were selling out day after day, and we were becoming more uncertain as to whether we had a real singer or not. Jesse then unfriended all of us on Facebook as well as blocked our phone numbers. In January of 2018, we received word that Jesse had died in an automobile collision. We don't know whether the collision was an accident or something else, all we knew is that our friend was gone.

We had his funeral in Wichita, KS shortly after and only had about

2 and a half weeks before we had to leave for tour. We had a tough decision to make: we could either turn down the opportunity and just try and figure out our futures, or we could fight to keep this band alive and utilize our creativity to pull this off within 2 and a half weeks.

The night of Jesse's funeral, we all talked about the bands future and decided to take the chance on making the tour happen, it was too big of an opportunity to just lay down and give up on. That night we put together a Craigslist ad (we had actually found Jesse the same way and figured we'd just lead with the platform we got results from) and got a multitude of responses back that evening.

We got a submission from a man named Vincent, who sang our song "My Disease" very well. He lived in Dallas, so we figured we'd set him up for an audition 2 days later. Vincent nailed the audition and was therefore invited back to a multitude of rehearsals that we had to fit in before this tour.

During rehearsals everything seemed to be going well and we were actually excited that we might have potentially found someone who was a great fit so soon, we even thought he had potential to be our permanent singer. We had about 30 minutes worth of material ready for the tour, it was perfect because that was how long our slotted set time was.

However, once we started to hit the road, all the problems that were dormant in rehearsals started to surface. For some reason, all of a sudden Vincent was having trouble remembering lyrics. Which didn't seem like a big problem because he brought a folder with all of the lyrics he needed in it, so we figured he'd iron out any kinks he had. Well the lyric issue didn't go away until about the last week of the tour.

Furthermore, Vincent was having trouble with his timing, and was coming in on sections a bar late or a bar early and was throwing us off. There were a couple times where Vincents screw ups were so bad and by consequence made us screw up so bad, that we almost came close to stopping. The drummer and I had to lock eyes to try and figure out how we were going to get back on track and finish the song. That tour felt like a bootcamp where we were going through a gig obstacle course.

To make matters worse, personality differences were starting to make themselves known and was starting to deteriorate the friendship we thought we initially had. Vincent went from a dedicated singer in the first weeks we knew him, to someone who was having trouble staying on time and remembering lyrics.

He never read the folder full of lyrics and began to treat this tour more like a vacation. He was also so focused on the fact that "we're going to write new music" that he neglected the songs he needed to know to make the set work. For him, this tour was the first of many, so if it wasn't perfect it was okay because this is just a warm-up run. For us, this was the culmination of years of hard work, networking, as well as learning things the hard way, and an opportunity to capitalize on the massive audiences we would be performing in front of.

It felt like a slap in the face, honestly. So we had to not only overcome the obstacle of losing our friend and singer then find a replacement in a short period of time, but now the obstacle of a singer who is having trouble performing the songs we rehearsed.

On top of that, Vincent had started to feel like his position as lead vocalist was locked in and we had to prevent him from finding out that by half way through the tour, we decided to move on from him after the tour. He told us that if he thought he would be done after the tour that he wouldnt have cared as much, so to maintain the shows quality even where it was, we had to keep this illusion up for him.

The tour went okay, we still gained lots of fans and sold some merch. However, we felt like we were performing at 60% capacity and felt like that while we did the best with what we had, we could've capitalized more.

So after all of these trials and tribulations, we were right back to where we started. No singer, gigs lined up, and not knowing what to do. The Nothing More tour with Vincent was February through the first week of March, and we had a gig with the band Puddle of Mudd 2 weeks later.

I ended up having to be the singer for that gig, which was definitely one of the bigger challenges of my musical career. Even though the gig went well, I definitely didn't want to do that forever nor did I have the vocal ability that the band needed to compliment its sound.

We took to Craigslist for now the third time to find a lead singer, and that is when we met our current singer. Gabriel. If you haven't figured out by this story, you shouldn't overlook Craigslist when trying to find band mates. Gabriel ended up coming in and blowing all of our minds. He took the bands sound to a level that it had never had the capabilities for in the past. We had finally found the singer that would compliment the band's sound even better than our original one.

The key to achieving your goals even in the face of all the obstacles is to be rigid on the result, but be flexible and creative with the strategies you use to get the results you want. How easy would it have been for my band and I to quit and just let that tour opportunity slip through our fingers? It would have certainly been easier than dealing with all the stress, expenses, and time it took to make that tour work.

However, our commitment to making this band work and have our name known was too strong to let anything stop us. This is the kind of determination you will need to have whenever things get tough, and they will get tough. I thought for a moment that I might have seen the end of my band, but because we viewed our problems as opportunities we were able to flex our creative muscles and get ourselves back on the right track within 4 months.

Your creativity should always be viewed as something that can give you a competitive edge compared to the other artists around you. Peter Drucker, one of the worlds top business leaders, said there was only 2 ingredients to a successful business: innovation and marketing. You might of guessed it already, but both of those two things are dependent on one thing…your creativity. I would also add to this, curiosity.

Curiosity actually comes from wanting to find out the answers to something. Most people are uncurious, easily bored, easily distracted, and as a consequence do not exercise their full potential. If you're curious as to *how* you can get something done, your brain will start to come up with ways in which that problem could potentially be solved.

If you however are uncurious, your brain won't really care about the answers to the question and therefore not work very hard to figure out a solution. This will kill your ability to innovate and grow because you will be in a constant reactionary state, where you are only curious about solving a problem when it requires your immediate attention.

Anticipation is probably the most important skill any entrepreneur or business owner can have because when you're curious about what will happen when certain markets slow down, when disruptive technology is introduced, etc., you'll be more likely to think of ways you can pivot and adapt to the environment instead of just waiting for the environment to change to your desires.

There is a wonderful book called "Who Moved My Cheese?" by Spencer Johnson that demonstrates the importance of anticipation and adapting to your circumstances. There are these mice that have been used to getting cheese from a specific place for a long time, but one day, the cheese is gone. Oh no! What do the mice do?

Well most of the mice sit around and wait for the cheese to come back, the others decide to go out into the unknown and look for the cheese. Which group of mice would you be in this situation? You were so used to getting your cheese from this one reliable spot and now its no longer reliable and you're confused.

How do you respond to that? If you're like most of the mice, you sit around and wait because that is what is most comfortable to you. It's what you've done forever and there is no way that the cheese could possibly be gone. If you're like the other mice, you understand that this problem isn't self-evidently going to go away. You have no idea whether the cheese is coming back, and you're afraid you could starve waiting around for the cheese to come back.

So you start to come up with strategies to get yourself to that cheese and all the different places it might have moved to. Your brain starts to open up as you now have pushed yourself into a situation where your curiosity is peaked. It's peaked because you're in a life or death situation. Being uncurious could mean death if you're the mice. In the music business, not looking for where the cheese went could mean the end of your band or project.

To compare it to my story I just told you, once Jesse passed away, the cheese moved. We could've sat around and complained about how the cheese was no longer where it's always been. We could've given up and waited for someone to find us "whenever the time was right".

We didn't do that though, we understood that the cheese had moved and the only way to survive was to go find where it had moved. As quick as we found some more cheese, it was gone again and we had to go out yet again to look for more cheese. Hopefully the analogy is painfully clear by this point, but the point here is that you cannot close off your creativity and ingenuity when the "cheese" moves.

This move is going to happen to you multiple times throughout your career, and so you need to be able to pivot when these things happen.

Conclusion

Putting It All Together

You've probably had a lot of changes throughout this book, and hopefully they're all for the better! It's not easy to burn away past beliefs we thought previously true, and I commend you for being the type of person that can hear all different kinds of information, even if you were initially hesitant.

Now it's time to take all this information and start figuring out how you can apply it in your own life. Knowledge without application will never transcend into wisdom, you have to start taking action to really get the most out of this.

I'm going to separate this closing for two different types of people. The first will be the average musician who has always been really into the art but not so much into the business. The second will be for the musicians who got into this because they were thinking more of the success and music became more secondary.

For Artists Who Were All About The Art

For my artists who really love the craft of music, one of the first things I would do is start expanding your education about business-itself. Trust me, this can be extremely exciting stuff once you really start getting the fundamental strategies. It gives you a sense of certainty that you know what you're supposed to be doing and what you should not be doing. Heck if you don't know what to do, at least learn what not to do, and then start by not doing any of those things.

Think about it like you're learning the skills you'll need to be independent and profitable because that's exactly what you're doing! You're separating yourself as someone who takes their future seriously.

You'll be far ahead of everyone else making the fatal mistakes that end up sinking their music business ship. Outside of what not to do, I would pay no more attention to convention than necessity demands. Shake things up, try new things, be different!

Use that creativity to be your edge in your music business. Remember this rule, "do what most people do, get what most people get". It's time for you to unleash the same creativity you put into your music into your business!

I remember how much easier it was for me to be behind the merch table when I knew how to sell versus before when I was just winging it and hoping that I said the right things or hoping people would buy.

I remember how much easier it was to start booking shows once I had a system that had been shown to me by a couple big time booking agents.

You will have similar experiences because once you start to take your music business seriously and understand that only you can do something about your success, you will you start to get skills that will greatly serve you.

On top of growing your skills, you're going to need a team around you that can help you get stuff done. No one builds anything great by themselves, it always comes down to having a team and a family that you can count on in a business of sharks.

The first people I would recommend getting on your team would be crew. Tour managers, drivers, merch people, technicians, engineers, etc. These are the people that are worth the most money you can spend on your team.

I have seen first hand, the difference between a camp that is run like a well-oiled machine, and a camp that is struggling all night to keep the shows head above water. Every single time without question, it came down to the quality of the crew.

Sometimes great crew are given crap systems, and still they find ways to adjust the bad system to make the show better, and if the band is smart, takes the advice. I've seen one man run guitar and bass with 17 total instruments to manage for the show due to the tuning changes.

We call him "Frosty", and Frosty is the definition of a professional. He has system after system that he runs through effortlessly to make a show run like butter. Not to mention he's an amazing dude who is a blast to hang around. When you find these people in your life or in your business, stay in touch.

This industry can be full of some really great people if you're willing to associate yourself with the right people. If you find people that are anything like Frosty, make friendships and learn everything you can. Be a sponge willing to learn then secrets of the trade.

I can tell you that some of the best memories I have in my music business is being associated with professionals like Frosty. I could literally fill this entire book with some pretty amazing people that I've been blessed to work with.

I say that not to brag, but to show you that there are good people out there, you just have to be willing to look for them and be open to see them. I know this industry is filled with people that are looking to take advantage of you, believe me, I've been ripped off before.

However, if you're willing to audit who you associate with and start associating with the people that are where you want to be, act they way you want to act, and treat others the way you'd want to be treated, then you're going to have a wonderful career full of some amazing memories.

For Artists Who Were All About The Money

Now, for the artists that got into this game because they wanted fame and fortune, understand that it is possible to be prosperous in this business. However, if you can focus on bringing value to people's lives more than the money, the money will be more likely to follow. If you can focus on finding who exactly the people you want to serve are and the best way to serve them, the money will be more likely to follow.

This business preys on hopeful artists who are looking for the glamour and shiny objects the industry knows it can use to manipulate artists into doing what they want. They're looking for the artists out there with that Hail Mary mindset and they're coming up with every trick in the book to get paid at your expense.

If there is one thing I'd recommend artists in this category do is think more intensely about the value they're bringing to their existing fans as well as what would be valuable to someone who isn't a fan just yet. Because from there you will be able to actually start to have a business that is sustainable.

Having new fans come into your world on a consistent basis is one of the keys to your business success. I remember one mentor I had said that the way he could determine with almost 100% accuracy who was going to be successful in any business was by one thing. The people who were not going to be successful were the people that were too focused on the actual acquiring of the money.

The ones who were actually going to be successful were the ones who focused on the marketing of the thing they're actually offering. When you start to become obsessed with the marketing of your music and your brand, you will start to have more success because marketing is really about identifying who people are and how you can serve them better.

The more you make this about serving as opposed to selling, you will build such goodwill that you will inevitably get supporters once you build a sales process. You are obviously in business to make money, but the money is a byproduct of the level to which someone feels understood and served. Don't focus on the money, focus on the marketing and how to get better at it.

The core of marketing is social and mass psychology, but not to the level of needing an undergraduate or degree in anything. Seriously, most things we need to know are pretty simple structurally and conceptually. Yes, the nitty gritty details matter, but a lot of stress over the little things is unhelpful.

Jim Rohn once said "Learn how to separate the majors and the minors. A lot of people don't do well simply because they major in minor things." (no musical pun intended). What are the major aspects of your business? Your fans, your music, your sales process, and your marketing are what I would consider the core "majors" of your business.

The "majors" of your business are things that move the needle. Getting more fans is a sign of growth or lack of growth. The more fans you're getting on a consistent basis, the more success you will have in your music business. The more music you're able to create and release, the more content you will have for your fans to consume and become more and more raving fans. The sales process is how you take all the people that have been your fans and listening to your music, and you actually start to convert followers into supporters. If you have nothing but followers and no way to monetize that following, then you're leaving money on the table, a lot of money. Finally, the marketing is how you start to acquire new fans so that you can start this whole process over. You get more fans from your marketing so that you can show them more of your music, so you can hopefully ascend them in your value ladder and through your sales process.

The "minors" of your business would be things that do not move the needle in your music business, and in the grand scheme of things don't matter as much as the "majors". Things like follower counts, what instrument you should use for a song, how long rehearsal should be, how to get in-ear monitors like "real" bands, etc. These are things that have their merit, sure, but don't really move the needle to make your music career happen. You need to have a way to get your minors taken care of, certainly, but you don't need to wrap all your focus up in the daily or weekly tasks for your band.

So to all my fellow artists out there, there is a lot we have covered inside of this book. I want you to think of this book like a resource that sits on your shelf, ready to help you whenever you need a refresher on some of these concepts. You've hopefully had a lot of ah-ha moments throughout this book, but I want to leave you with a couple final thoughts.

Throughout my career I've seen so many different trends come and go as well as the attitudes and behaviors on the ground floor of the business, and through this journey I want you to know that the people who are on the top or have success are not smarter than you. A lot of them either put in the work and understand this business or they're riding the wave of an industry that is dying.

I know that sounds harsh, but I see some people trying to model and do things the way some of their favorite bands do it, not understanding that their favorite band may be operating within a system that is dying and antiquated. This leads to confusion because we start saying things like "well, (insert a big artist you enjoy) is on a record label so maybe I just need to get on the same label".

This is NOT how you will start to become an entrepreneur and model success. That will suck you up into the same system that is spitting bands out poorer than before with little to know value provided to them. I understand it may be tempting to see one of your favorite legacy acts or even modern acts that are still very much in the system, and think *that* is how I'm going to make it.

You need to understand that setting up a successful music career is like baking a cake. You have to the *right* ingredients in the *right* order at the *right* time or else your cake (and your business) is going to turn out like complete shit. Yes, working with a label *might* be a viable option at some point in your career, but is that how you're going to get your big break? Hell no!

The right vehicle you want to be in that will take you to your destination with all the ownership of your music and your profits in tact, is becoming a music entrepreneur. I hope inside this book, I've given you some amazing principles to help guide you through this dilemma artists face when first becoming music entrepreneurs.

However, your education is not over. There is still plenty more to learn, and I'm certain each new thing you learn along this journey will add a little bit more fire to your music career so you can start to ignite and blow up! The stuff you will learn will be as new at first as I'm sure some of the concepts here in this books might have been.

The best part is you are totally capable of learning and implementing this knowledge. How many times have you heard about some music theory concept that sounds crazy, but then you learn the principles and all of a sudden it all clicks? That's what its like when you begin your entrepreneur education. You're going to get a golden nugget here, and another one there, and each time you're going to be getting puzzle pieces to fit together and create a successful thriving music business.

If you're ever in a situation where people or jobs start to try and hold you back from becoming a professional, remember the principles, the lessons, and the stories inside this book. There will be an experience when you start to ascend up your goals where it feels like people close to you may be potentially trying to hold you back.

You might have heard of crab-in-the-bucket syndrome. It's where people will knowingly, or sometimes unknowingly, will try and prevent you from ascending to the next phase in your life because they're comfortable with who you are now. Some people will like you because they can easily put you in a box and when you start to break that mold people will either distance themselves or try and bring you down. This is basically an attempt at sabotage, which like I said, could be done on a conscious or unconscious level.

Don't take it too personally, sometimes people will try to persuade you to do what they did. Unless you want to live their life, I would take their opinon with the fattest grain of salt imaginable. Abraham Lincoln once said, "I learn from everybody, even if it's sometimes what *not* to do". Take these naysayers and cynics words as simply how *not* to look at something.

The game is closed off to the people who will not even put the effort necessary to play it. *This* is your advantage. This age we live in is filled with so many people that are so scared about failure that they won't even risk taking the first step. They get to say "At least I didn't fail" as they shout from the stands they had to pay a premium to come see you, the artist willing to put in the work. Theodore Rosevelt once said "it is not the critic who counts; not the man who points out how the strong man stumbles, or where the doer of deeds could have done them better. The credit belongs to the man who is actually in the arena, whose face is marred by dust and sweat and blood; who strives valiantly; who errs, who comes short again and again, because there is no effort without error and shortcoming; but who does actually strive to do the deeds; who knows great enthusiasms, the great devotions; who spends himself in a worthy cause; who at the best knows in the end the triumph of high achievement, and who at the worst, if he fails, at least fails while daring greatly, so that his place shall never be with those cold and timid souls who neither know victory nor defeat."

You will have moments of blood, sweat, and tears, but you are in a rough business. You will beat out your competition simply by sticking around and consistently growing. I've met plenty of artists who were more talented than me, but they didn't care to learn the business so they are the ones that eventually quit the game. It simply takes recognition of what you know, and what you don't know, and committing to closing the gap. What skills in business are you lacking right now? What areas of your art could be improved by honing your craft?

Once you Identify these gaps, you will be able to start seeing some progress because you will become well-rounded in your approach to your music career. While most are out there questioning whether they can do it, whether they're "selling out" or not, whether learning more about business is a scam, or whatever excuse they come up with next. You will be out there taking your place and gathering your audience and sharing your creativity and message with the world. I sincerely hope you will take this as a call to action to go out and start to build that music business, get educated, get going, and never looking back. I'm sure as hell glad I never looked back!

In Summary

So what was the musician's dilemma? It was the dilemma of whether or not to commit to becoming a professional in the music business because we were unsure of whether we could make it a career or not, and we didn't know how to balance our art and our business. Hopefully by now, your dilemma will be resolved.

You now know that there are a lot of different artists out there who are walking around with myths in their head holding them back from their goals. Myths like believing that aiming for success or even using common practice business strategies are somehow "selling out". You know that phrase doesn't even mean what people are using it to describe and the whole idea is built out of envious artists, greedy music publishing companies and instrument manufacturing companies.

We debunked the myth that if you want something right, you have to do it yourself. Nothing great is built alone. On top of that, having a team that you trust around you that can actually fulfill your business systems will be one of the greatest assets in your life. They will be able to replace all the work you would normally have to do essentially being a small business owner. If there is one thing more valuable than money, it's time. Old billionaires would give away every cent they have if it meant they could have youth or time back. Never forget that.

You also discovered the idea that if you build something, people will come is a complete myth. There is no reason to think people will come unless you give them a reason to or attract them to your music somehow. It's all in the marketing. It's not the best product that wins, it's the most known product. McDonalds is not the best burger place in the world, but it's the most known burger place in the world. As a consequence, McDonalds is worth $21,000,000,000 and you can find them on almost any corner.

There is nothing that leads to more frustration for artists than putting months of work into something, and then once everything is all finalized, no one even hears it. I don't want that to happen to you because it's an awful feeling. It's not because there is anything wrong with what you're offering, but it's probably the way you're marketing what you have to offer. Commit to becoming passionate about the marketing of your music and you will start to grow because you will become more known. Unrecognized genius is practically a cliché, no excuses in today's age not to be unknown. Anyone can spend $100 or $1,000 on an ad and get known by somebody.

However, the most pervasive myth that you will avoid is the idea that success will make you a bad songwriter. There are so many misconceptions about how artists can create consistently, which is ultimately where this myth comes from. The cases of the artist who got big writing about how things in their life are awful, but now they're famous and have money so they can't dig as much from that same well anymore for songwriting. As a result, they tend to put out stale, uninspired music.

On a side note, there is always a ton of ways to get into a creative state at will. You don't need to resort to alcohol. You don't need to resort to hard drugs. Counter to what you might have heard about writing great songs, drugs to do not make you write better songs. If anything, drugs have held back legends from writing more of the great music we know and love. You could see how someone who is having problems writing can make things a lot worse because they thought drugs would make them more creative, but instead it locked them up and ruined their lives.

Once you get passed these myths, you learned what unhealthy unbalance versus healthy unbalance actually looks like and why you want some healthy unbalance. More importantly, you know that the common pitfalls of artists are not only in their psychology but in their approaches to getting results. You learned the pitfalls of being all about the art and resisting any kind of business implementation into your music career.

You know that it's not about just writing songs and letting "industry professionals" take care of your responsibilities. It's about adapting to the digital age and becoming open to the idea that business is okay and will be the way that we take a passion of ours and turn it into something you can make a career. It's great to be passionate about art, but we now know that becoming an entrepreneur will help you really ignite your music business.

You know the downfall of artists who are all about the money, and while they maybe got into this business with sincerity, have turned their relationship with music into a job and now view it basically no different than a 9-5. You know that while it's important to stay busy, you don't want to turn your art into a job. Keep creating music on a regular basis and you will stay inspired, you keep creating systems in your music business and you will stay free.

Once you bring those two perspectives together, you will start to find balance between your art and your business. You learned about the yin and the yang analogy to your art and your business, and how each side has positive and negative characteristics. It's now time for you to start taking this balance and go deeper down into the details. You learned how to balance the art that is within your business as well as how to balance the business that is within your art. Some people may see that and claim word salad, but you know this has a real relationship to your music business.

You understand that business is actually a creative and artistic pursuit, and even though business is considered very number-based, black and white thing, you can use all your creative skills to help make progress happen inside your music career. It's often said that businesses that build themselves on innovation go bankrupt on the conventional. People get started and adapt easily as they have momentum moving towards a goal, but get stuck in their ways of how they've always done it. You learned how to stay adaptive and keep a nice balance of art inside your business.

Finally, you learned how to balance the business that is within your art. You know that art has been a commodity for a long time, and there are people who are definitely willing to support you. You will find fans who will be so excited about your music and find it so valuable that they will literally part with their money to keep you creating music. There are many ways you will find to monetize your music, start to think about the value you can provide to your fans, and if you get stuck, imagine that you're creating a product for your favorite band and it's for you. You will start to think of tons of ways you can create valuable products for your fans.

Now you not only have a way to avoid becoming to one sided, but you also have a way to use each side effectively within each other. You learned to balance the yin with the yang, but also the yin within the yang as well as the yang within the yin. This is the same concept as balancing not only your art with your business, but also the business with the art. Now you can start to take action without hesitation.

In the movie *The Karate Kid*, Daniel is painting Miyagi's fence, sanding his floor, and waxing his car. Daniel become angered because *he* thought he was going to be learning about karate in a specific way. However, when Daniel goes to learn from Miyagi, he finds himself confused as to if he's even learning karate at all or if Miyagi is just benefiting from some free child labor. As Miyagi demonstrated, Daniel had not only been covertly learning Karate, but was actually proficient at it. Enough that he could block Miyagi's kicks and punches having seemingly never practiced karate.

When it comes to learning about the music business, it will often feel like how Daniel felt in the beginning when he was doing things he felt had no bearing on karate, when in actuality, he was learning the fundamentals that would serve him in the future. This is true when becoming an entrepreneur, you will be learning things that you may feel are not making any difference, when actually you are going through the things that will sharpen and serve you all throughout your life.

You're no longer held down by falsehoods and myths and you're now equipped with the perspective you will need to start to make progress in the music business. This business, like any business, is open to anyone who is willing to learn the secrets and willing to take action on this knowledge. The people that have the most success are the ones that understand exactly how to set up their business. They have a foundation they can rely on. They understand not only the big picture concepts I've talked about in this book, but they understand the principles of selling and marketing.

In the next installment of the Musicians Trilogy, you're going to discover exactly the strategies, the tactics, the numbers, and everything you're going to need to know to not only set up a music business, but set up a business that makes money and creates the kind of freedom every artist out there is looking for from their music career. If you're ready to start learning how to effortlessly influence and attract your dream fans and how you can make a career, go to <u>www.MusiciansEnterprise.com</u> and get a free copy today, just cover shipping and I'll send a copy to your door.

End Notes

Preface

1. Volpenhiem, Sarah. "One person dead in two-car crash outside Marion", *Marion Star.* January 17, 2018, https://www.marionstar.com/story/news/local/2018/01/17/one-person-dead-two-car-crash-outside-marion/1040216001/
2. Wilson, Rain. *The Office.* DVD. Directed by Ken Kwapis. Los Angeles: NBC Universal Television, 2007.

Introduction

3. KIRRA. "KIRRA - Sixteen Suns (official audio)", *YouTube.* February 7, 2019, https://www.youtube.com/watch?v=1yAUGZvKgWU
4. Robertson, Cliff. *Spiderman.* DVD. Directed by Sam Raimi. New York City: Marvel Enterprises, 2002.

4 Harmful Myths

Myth #1

5. *Bar Rescue,* "Big Sisters Watching", Paramount Global, November 8, 2015.
6. Wall Street Journal. "will.i.am on How to Make Money with Music", *YouTube.* May 17, 2013, https://www.youtube.com/watch?v=vHNiigP0ck0

Myth #2

7. Gerber, Michael. *The 'E' Myth: Why Most Small Businesses Don't Work and What To Do About It.* Harper Collins Publishing, 1995
8. The Founder. DVD. Directed by John Lee Hancock. FilmNation Entertainment, 2016.
9. Kroc, Ray. Grinding It Out. Henry Regnery Company, 1977.

Myth #3

10. Spotify. *Loud and Clear.* March 18, 2021, https://loudandclear.byspotify.com/
11. Call of Duty 4. Developed by Infinity Ward. Published by Activision, November 5, 2007.
12. Assassins Creed. Developed by Ubisoft Montreal. Published by Ubisoft, November 13, 2007.
13. Assassins Creed II. Developed by Ubisoft Montreal. Published by Ubisoft, November 17, 2009.
14. Assassins Creed Brotherhood. Developed by Ubisoft Montreal. Published by Ubisoft, November 16, 2010.
15. Assassins Creed Revelations. Developed by Ubisoft Montreal. Published by Ubisoft, November 15, 2011.
16. Assassins Creed III. Developed by Ubisoft Montreal. Published by Ubisoft, October 30, 2012.
17. Guitar Hero: Metallica. Developed by Neversoft. Published by Activision, March 26, 2009.

Myth #4

18. Social Network. DVD. Directed by David Fincher. Columbia Pictures, 2010.
19. Office Space. DVD. Directed by Mike Judge. 20th Century Fox, 1999.
20. The Founder. DVD. Directed by John Lee Hancock. FilmNation Entertainment, 2016.
21. Fight Club. DVD. Directed by Directed by David Fincher. 20th Century Fox, 1999.
22. Wall Street. DVD. Directed by Oliver Stone. 20th Century Fox, 1987.
23. KIRRA. "KIRRA - Flesh Gives Way (official)", YouTube. April 20, 2022, https://www.youtube.com/watch?v=rbEUbIoDlvI
24. Nietzsche, Frederich. Twilight of the Idols. Hackett Publishing Company, Inc., 1889.

PART ONE

25. Chamorro-Premuzic, Tomas. "Are Successful People More Neurotic?", Forbes. https://www.forbes.com/sites/tomaspremuzic/2022/06/07/are-successful-people-more-neurotic/?sh=3c46d8ea5860
26. Peterson, Dr. Jordan. Understand Myself Personality Test. https://understandmyself.com/
27. Kibeom Lee, Ph.D., & Michael C. Ashton, Ph.D. HEXACO Personality Test. https://hexaco.org/hexaco-online
28. Drumeo. "Thomas Lang: Applying Technique On The Drum-Set - Drum Lesson (Drumeo)", YouTube. May 9, 2015, https://www.youtube.com/watch?v=Tia3nieOu0o
29. Seneca. Our Groundless Fears. 64 BCE, Loeb Classical Library, 1917.

30. Aaron Moreno. "Metallica, Lady Gaga Moth Into Flame MIC Feed", YouTube. February 14, 2017, https://www.youtube.com/watch?v=Y4Jb17V0a4Q

All About the Art

31. Buffett, Warren. ""
32. TEDx Talks. "Why I read a book a day (and why you should too): the law of 33% | Tai Lopez | TEDxUBIWiltz", YouTube. https://www.youtube.com/watch?v=7bB_fVDlvhc

All About the Money

33. Dick Mittens. "John Mayer Teaching at Berklee College of Music (Full Berklee Clinic 2008)", YouTube. November 14, 2008, https://www.youtube.com/watch?v=LRmrMDfWkNo

PART TWO

34. Nothing More. "This Is The Time (Ballast)", *Nothing More.* Eleven Seven, 2014.
35. Drum Program. "Chris Coleman Clinic", *YouTube.* May 18, 2016, https://www.youtube.com/watch?v=y46skGXRbWU
36. Robbins, Anthony. "Discover The 6 Human Needs" 2014, https://www.tonyrobbins.com/mind-meaning/do-you-need-to-feel-significant/
37. Bee Gees. "Stayin' Alive", Saturday Night Fever. RSO, 1977.
38. Bee Gees. "One", One. Warner Bros Records, 1989.
39. Alexis Romero. "How Sia and her songwriter come up with new single", *YouTube.* August 3, 2014, https://www.youtube/59nwMeoYCkQ
40. Cavuoto, Robert. "Interview With Mark Tremonti (Guitars, Vocals) (Tremonti, Alter Bridge)". Apr 17, 2016, https://myglobalmind.com/2016/04/17/interview-mark-tremonti-guitars-vocals-tremonti-alter-bridge/
41. Holmes, Chet. *Ultimate Sales Machine.* Penguin Publishing Group, 2008.

Balancing Art with Business

42. Beyonce Legion. *Twitter.* March 14, 2018, https://twitter.com/BeyLegion/status/973912605088731136?ref_src=twsrc%5Etfw%7Ctwcamp%5Etweetembed%7Ctwterm%5E973912605088731136%7Ctwgr%5E%7Ctwcon%5Es1_&ref_url=https%3A%2F%2Fwww.popbuzz.com%2Fmusic%2Fartists%2Fbeyonce%2Fjay-z-on-the-run-2-tour-prices-twitter-reactions%2F
43. Vai, Steve. Evo Tour Packages. https://www.vai.com/evo-packages-us/

Balancing Business with Art

44. Tony Robbins. "Steve Wynn Shares his Ultimate Competitive Edge at Business Mastery", *YouTube.* October 29, 2012, https://www.youtube/bHnETMBYh7E
45. Hendrix, Jimi. *Life.* October 3, 1969.
46. John Thornburgh. "Nothing More Bass Solo @ Rockfest Kansas City 2014", *YouTube.* June 1, 2014, https://www.youtube.com/watch?v=JA2CyOyFXnY

Closing

47. Roosevelt, Theodore. *Citizens In A Republic.* Paris, France: April 23, 1910.
48. The Karate Kid. DVD. Directed by Directed by John G. Avildsen. Columbia Pictures, 1984.

Acknowledgments

I want to acknowledge all the people who made this book possible and every single one of you who have supported me on this journey. I want to thank my wife Madison, who has literally been a never ending source of support and has always inspired me to become the best husband and father I can possibly be. I want to thank my family for helping me get my career started when I had nothing. I want to thank my band members who have been great friends and always helped me through the hills and valleys of my life and our career. I want to thank all my mentors who have helped me obtain and maintain progress in my business, without their guidance, I'm not sure where I would be. I want to thank all my fans and supporters whether it be for my band KIRRA or Musician Mastery and any of it's associated brands. It is with your support that I m able to fulfill my purpose and serve musicians to help solve the dilemma of how to balance their art and their business as well as how to end the uncertainty of our futures and our careers. I knew that when I started this journey that all the black eyes from the business and all the lessons I had to learn the hard way were not in vain, and in fact could be shared and be used to generate some good for other musicians out there. If you get any value from my books, courses or free videos so that you can improve your life and get you where you want, then I've done good work. Because that is the measure of my success in my eyes, the value I'm able to bring people and the impact it can have on their lives.

About The Author

Daxton is an entrepreneur, investor, musician, and instructor/coach who has spent more than 4,000+ hours working 1-on-1 with musicians to help them revolutionize their musical, personal, and financial lives on and off the stage with his company <u>Musician Mastery</u>. Daxton is also the guitarist and songwriter for the hard rock band <u>KIRRA</u> who has sold tens of thousands in merch sales as well as over hundreds of thousands of streams on all streaming platforms worldwide. "This is what I've dedicated my life to is serving entrepreneurs and music entrepreneurs more specifically, and from this path I've been able to help many artists all over the world become more like entrepreneurs in their music business. If you're one of those people that have enjoyed this book or want to get more training on exactly how to build a music business with all its major supporters in place, go to <u>MusiciansIgnite.com</u> and check out my coaching program that goes into everything you're going to need to know to start making things happen.

Printed in the United States
by Baker & Taylor Publisher Services